Dance
FOR YOUR LIFE

Sue Hewgill Peterson

The right of Sue Hewgill Peterson to be identified as the Author of this work has been asserted in accordance with the Copyright, Designs and Patents Act 1988.

British Library Cataloguing in Publication Data.
A catalogue record for this book is available from the British Library.

ISBN 978-1-7396523-0-2

Umbrella
EDITIONS

I firmly believe that we need dance now more than ever. We need to find ways of bringing people together again, of improving their mental and physical health and of celebrating what it means to be alive. To dance is to live. Dance does all of this and more.

This book demonstrates to teachers all over the world that they are not only teaching their own dance genre but they are also giving their pupils so many hidden transferable life skills. Through teaching dance we're creating lifelong behaviours, mindsets and passions. Dance widens access to the benefits and wellbeing that this incredible artform can offer everyone.

Tim Arthur
Chief Executive, Royal Academy of Dance
Global Headquarters, London

Contents

About the author

Sue's dance journey began at three when she attended ballet classes in her hometown of Hartlepool, UK. She gained a place at Elmhurst Ballet School aged ten, in Camberley, Surrey (the school has since relocated to Birmingham, England) and progressed to train at the Royal Ballet School, London.

Sue has had many exciting roles in the world of dance: from establishing her own dance studio and dancewear shop, which continues to run today, under new management, to working as the Head of Dance at Queen Margaret's Independent Boarding School in York, UK. She also taught for The Royal Ballet School's Associate Programme. Her love of dance is infectious, influencing hundreds of new dancers, many of whom have established careers in the profession.

She has performed in and choreographed many musicals and ballets and staged countless amateur and professional productions including pieces set to music composed especially for her.

She was a Committee Member, Treasurer and Vice Chair of The Yorkshire Region of the Royal Academy of Dance (RAD) and has run and taught prestigious Summer Schools for the RAD and Yorkshire Youth Dance Theatre, for schools in Spain, Isle of Man and America. She is honoured to be a Life Member of The Royal Academy of Dance.

Between 2004 and 2010 Sue lived and worked in North Carolina USA, passionately sharing her expertise as the Executive Director of Carolina

Performing Arts Centre. In that post, she introduced the Royal Academy of Dance Graded and Vocational Examination System to Eastern North Carolina.

Sue returned to the USA in 2015, this time to Florida. She volunteered with *The Sarasota Ballet* company, and in 2018 was employed as Head of the Children's Programme, teaching *The Royal Academy of Dance* syllabus. In September 2020 she and her husband returned to England.

Inspired by teaching classes and workshops virtually in the USA, Sue set up a Zoom room at home from where she continues to teach ballet through learning online.

Sue is an active volunteer and philanthropist. Her voluntary roles have included rehearsing shows with *Carolina Ballet* in Raleigh USA; stewarding at the BBC *Antiques Roadshow*; The Royal Ballet School's Junior School, White Lodge in Richmond Park, Surrey, UK.

Sue's philanthropic work extends to her role as Founder and President of the 'We Can Dance' charity which raises money to enable children with Special Needs in the North of England to attend weekly dance classes and holiday workshops. Profits from the sale of this book will go to supporting it's work.

She is a volunteer at Thomas Gainsborough's House Art Museum in Sudbury, Suffolk, UK, where she lives. Sue shares her wealth of dance knowledge through her talk *Dance keeps me on my toes* and via virtual courses such as *Let's Pointe to Safety*. She also holds in-studio classes in her home town as a licensed *Silver Swans* teacher. This is a worldwide initiative devised by The Royal Academy for the over 55s. She also bakes a mean pumpkin pie.

Website:- www.suehewgillpeterson.com

Testimonials

Anne Walker MBE: businesswoman, dance teacher, speaker, mentor & best-selling author.

I am delighted that Sue has written this book highlighting many of the thoughts that I have regarding how dance gives us so much in our lives. I particularly like the emphasis on children's outcomes and how teachers impact on the lives of so many children and transform lives.

Dance teachers should be applauded and celebrated. So much more than just a teacher – they are almost a substitute parent to many of their students, as they are role models, mentors and social workers, offering support, stability and a disciplined approach to life. They instil a love of dance, music and theatre which will hopefully turn many students into tomorrow's theatregoers, if not performers or teachers.

It was my dance teachers who taught me to strive for something better and the determination to achieve my dreams. They made me believe in myself. They taught me to keep on working and striving and they were there for support when things were tough. They also taught me there was so much more to learn about dance, which is such a blueprint for life than mere 'steps'!

Most dance teachers do not realise the vitally important role they play in our society, and they are often unaware of the massive impact they have on the lives of so many young people. And so I say to dance teachers everywhere – over the years of running your school you have created many poised, disciplined, well-mannered young people, and because of you they will go through life understanding how to work as a team, realise that through hard work and diligent practice anything is possible and know that dreams really can come true.

So let us celebrate and applaud dance educators everywhere. Let us share our knowledge, our professionalism and our passion with each other so that, eventually, dance teachers everywhere will be respected as the hugely important professionals within society that they actually are.

https://www.annewalker.com

Sandra Burnham, Examiner of the Royal Academy of Dance - Monterey, California, U.S.A.

I have known Sue Peterson for more than thirty years as a colleague and teacher of great distinction and accomplishment. I am delighted that she has used the strange time of Covid-19 seclusion to bring her great love and knowledge of dance to inform this book, incorporating the joy of movement and offering a liberation of mind and body to its readers. No matter what the readers' dance interest or knowledge may be, here is richness and inspiration. Enjoy...

Testimonial from Kathi Doepfner, Florida, USA, who attends adult ballet class

I ABSOLUTELY LOVED READING Dance for your Life

These are thoughts that are always in my mind.

Example - feeling insecure in a class or not good enough - or my body doesn't look as good as I would like it to look.

Sometimes I have to remind myself that when I started taking a 'class' I was 30 years old. Not being the most confident person in the world, I am even surprised that I lasted all these years. I was never exposed to dance as a child. A friend of mine suggested we try it. So, why would I put up with all these insecurities if I didn't love it!!!

Even today, when I attend a class that frustrates me, why is my first reaction - I can't wait to take my next class. Maybe I will do better. It has to be love...

Your observations in the book are all things that anyone can relate to. I suffer at times from being anxious (mostly coming from family problems). Once I take my place at the barre, I am in the only place in the world I want to be at that moment. I can go into the class feeling anxious or nervous about something and by the end of class I can take on the world.

Additionally, I liked seeing the different illustrations, they are inspiring.

I could go on and on. This book is my Bible.

Testimonial from Lynn Gregory MA, educator and trainer, mentor, public speaker, consultant

I think you have an amazing book. Throughout, your passion, enthusiasm, and professionalism shine through. Your great wealth of experience and expertise add weight to a very important part of life affecting everyone and every aspect – personal, work, relationships, family.

We need all the ammunition we can get to prevent government and education policy makers debasing and pushing the arts into their 'frivolous' category. The arts are essential to life. Movement is key to learning.

Introduction

I believe dance can change your life. It certainly impacted mine, and the lives of many of the people who have kindly shared their stories with me.

We know:

The world can change in a heartbeat!
So, your world can change in a *Dancebeat!!*

As we adapted to life in the Covid-19 global pandemic, I saw even more clearly the gifts dance gives us. I have been inspired by my students of all ages, who saw dance as a way to be kind to themselves, and to connect with others. Even when they were unable to leave their homes, their resourcefulness and commitment in holding onto dance offered dollops of normality and pleasure when the world was turned upside down.

But this book was in the making long before any of us heard of Covid-19. The idea first came about when I met fellow dancer and Elmhurst Ballet School alumna, Jessica Spencer-Keyse. Dancing has also played a vital role in Jessica's life, though it has moved in a different direction from mine – dance has led her to academic research, exploring the connection between arts and wellbeing. As we spoke, we realised just how many dormant transferable life skills and benefits dance had brought to our lives. We wanted to showcase these in a simple, clear way.

What you are reading now is the result. It's here for anyone interested in living well. Perhaps you have felt ill or low, or your children are looking for a new dimension to their lives. Perhaps dance has been on your radar as something to explore. Maybe you would like to bring more vitality into your life, or you are here driven by curiosity: what on earth has dance to do with living life better?

In any of the above scenarios, this book is for you.

The working title for the book was *The Dance Umbrella*. Let me explain...

When I was Head of Dance at Queen Margaret's Independant Boarding School, York, UK, I wanted to show my students the enormous range of dance options available, as many of them associated the movement solely with tutus and performance. I wanted them to see the many facets and styles of dance. So I drew an umbrella with the name of different dance genres hanging from each spoke.

That was the first dance umbrella, but since then, I have seen how dance can be an umbrella in so many other ways, building a community and inspiring confidence. It provides protection against life's storms, just like an umbrella, and equips us to go out into the world, whatever the weather. And like the best umbrellas, dance is joyful and colourful, bringing a smile to your face on a dreary day. To avoid confusion with the international London-based dance festival '*The Dance Umbrella*' which is celebrating 21st century choreography, it was decided to title the book *Dance for Your Life*.

This book, will teach how our lives can be elevated through dance. It offers us life skills to educational opportunities, new friendships and an opportunity for self-care, reaping physical and mental health benefits from moving to music! As a Life Member and ballet teacher of The Royal Academy of Dance, I have seen how dance transforms lives of young and old.

During the Covid-19 pandemic we all learned ways of keeping ourselves and others safe. People who had never gone for a run or

used YouTube to find a yoga or dance tutorial, gave it a go, relishing the opportunity for daily exercise. They realised how moving your body equates to feeling good. Some of these people have developed new habits for life.

In a world stripped back, we realised what's important. Dance has reconnected me with dear friends and introduced me to people from many walks of life – our paths would not have crossed otherwise. As I enjoy life in my seventies, dance is still opening up new international opportunities and friendships. I am heartened to observe young children, such as these pictured in the photo above in Florida, USA, becoming firm friends in the future through ballet classes.

I hope you too will see that dance is a gift for all; besides being a fun hobby, it will unlock mindfulness, fulfilment and happiness and better health.

In the process of writing this book, we asked 'friends' on Meta (formerly Facebook) for response to:

How has dance impacted on your life?

I hope their responses, which are incorporated here, will inspire you. You will read stories of people who found ways to express themselves through dance; turned their educational prospects around; regained self-worth and as an adult after years spent caring for others, brought the skills they had learned via dance to their successful careers. These stories are both ordinary and extraordinary; ordinary because these opportunities are open to anyone, not just those of us who show exceptional dance talent, and extraordinary because they have been truly life-changing experiences.

How to use this book

If you would rather dip in and out, feel free to do so. You will find stories, quotes and pictures throughout the book to inspire you on your journey. If you'd like to read it cover to cover, please do. The chapters will take you through a tour of dance's role in society across the globe. Look at the incredible skills and educational impact dance offers. Explore also all the ways dance benefits wellbeing. The final chapter advises how you can bring this all to life and get started.

Another objective of this book is to raise funds for, and bring awareness to the charity *We Can Dance* which I founded as *Charity Productions* in the mid-nineties. A group of children with special needs attended one of our performances, The Carnival of the Animals, with music by Camille Saint-Saëns. After the show, they asked their teacher 'Why can't we do that?'. So a summer school, based on the ballet *Still Life at the Penguin Café*, included them as well as other pupils. This was quickly followed by holiday workshops and ballet classes. The charity was registered in 2010, and now provides dance lessons to children with multiple and special needs all over the northeast of England.

I passionately believe that all children should have the chance to express themselves through dance. By subscribing to the philosophy of this book, you are helping in this vital work.

Thank you

NB. Since this book draws on my UK and US work spheres, life and influences both British English and American English are interspersly used.

Dance mind map

Adaptability

Learning how the body functions and moves

Kinaesthetic learning

Dreams

Concentration

Curiousity

Joy and fun

Non-competitive

Confidence

Spatial
awareness

Dance
family

Social
skills

Friends
for life

Discipline

Co-ordination

Musicality

Exercising
for a healthy
body and
mind

Chapter 1

Dance to live well

The world can change in a heartbeat!
Your world can change in a *Dancebeat!!*

**Dancing is the loftiest, the most moving, the most beautiful of the arts.
For it is no mere translation or abstraction of life. It is life itself.**

HENRY HAVELOCK (1859 – 1939), An English physician

Your Dancing Story

We all have different associations with the concepts of dance and dancing. For some of us, dance may be a source of personal joy. For others, it may be inspirational and wondrous to look at what highly trained professionals can do. For others still it may be a source of embarrassment, 'I can't dance' or 'Only children and drunk wedding guests dance'.

Take a few minutes to think about what dance means to you. Use a notebook and pen, if you can, and write down all the associations you have with dancing, from your earliest memory to now. Think about what the important people around you told you about dancing too.

Hopefully those few minutes helped you understand your personal dancing story. Because, whether we consider ourselves 'dancers' or not, dance is part of our world. It reaches us all, whether we have grown up with positive or negative attitudes to it.

Throughout this book you will find snippets of how dance has affected the lives of many people. When first embarking on research, people were asked to share their stories and there was an overwhelming response – from professionals, parents, and people for whom dance was a social lifeline. You will read some of their experiences in later chapters. Dance does touch us all.

Here are some of the ways dance can benefit you, and those around you. I want to share how I feel about the undercover story behind dance participation. The transferable underlying skills learned are many, as you will discover as you read on.

Your dancing life

This book has taken a brief look at some of the ways dance weaves through society, and the important role it plays in many aspects of

life. It goes into many of these in more detail in later chapters. But now it's time to get personal. At the start of the chapter, you were invited to look at your own preconceptions about dance.

We all have our histories with dance, as it is all around us – on the TV, with audiences tapping their feet to buskers on street corners, at social occasions, in community centres and school halls. Babies instinctively bop and wiggle to music. But perhaps we have shut ourselves off from the extra possibilities dance has to offer as we grow.

Here are some of the ways dance can benefit you, and those around you.

Self-care

For many people, dancing can be a way to switch off from the stresses of life and release tension. This is true of children just as much as adults – after school children often need an outlet to move their bodies and feel free. For adults, a weekly dance class can be a dose of much needed 'me-time' away from responsibilities for others.

Clare Meteer, an aspiring dancer, writes:

'As a three-year-old, my grandma signed me up for my first dance class. I could barely talk but wanted to keep going back! I fell in love. As I got older, I knew this was something I wanted to do for the rest of my life! I wanted to continue expressing my feelings through movement! As the oldest of six children in my family, it can be hard when you have to help with your younger siblings, and with school, you can get easily overwhelmed! I use dance as an outlet to take a break from all the stress outside of the dance studio. When I step into my dance studio, I immediately feel free, free from stress, free from all burdens of life! When I dance, I can let everything go! Dancing is my passion, and whether I make it as a professional or not, I will continue to dance until the day I die!'

Exercise

Anything that moves your body is valuable both for your fitness and your mental wellbeing, and the effect seems to be heightened by adding music and the playfulness of dance into the equation. Movement releases endorphins which are our body's natural stress relievers, meaning we tend to feel better after a dancing session. We are strengthening our heart, muscles and aerobic fitness at the same time.

While some of us may feel nervous (or terrified) at the thought of performing in front of others, performance brings unique rewards. It brings together training, rehearsal, working with others and offers a sense of satisfaction that many find addictive, whether on the community or international stage. It also reminds us that we have a choice in how we prepare ourselves for life – that we can choose how to present ourselves to the world, both on stage and off it. This is a vital piece of awareness in developing decision-making and self-confidence.

Toni Renée Taylor in Florida!

Music and dance compliment each other and are universal languages. Ex-UN Secretary General, Kofi Anan (1938 –2018) put it this way:

> *'In a world of diversity where often values clash, music leaps across language barriers and unites people of quite different cultural backgrounds. And so, through music, all peoples can come together to make the world a more harmonious place.'*

Dance deepens our understanding of music, both giving us pleasure, and access to another means to relax, express our creativity and celebrate life.

The dance artist and American Sign Language interpreter Brandon Kazen-Maddox shines a spotlight on how dance movements make music visible.

This is such an amazing concept. Dance movements making music visible. He says...

'There is a ports de bras, which you only learn from ballet, which I was really engraving into my body. As I watched, my sign language, which had been with me my whole life, became more visible with music.'

Personal expression

Sometimes we carry emotions we can't always express in words. Dance enables us to let out feelings, in turn releasing stress, but also helping us understand ourselves and each other better.

'Being a dancer has really made me the person I am today. Without ballet in my life I would be extremely lost. Dance has the power for you to express yourself emotionally without using words. You also have the potential to find yourself as a person through the roles you dance.'

GINA SCOTT
Semperoper Ballet, Dresden, Germany.

Dancer and dance teacher Claire Norman also turned to dance to help with communication and expressing views and feelings:

'As someone who has stammered since the age of five, I learned to invest in dance to communicate when I struggled with my speech. Maybe this is

what provoked me to learn dance styles such as hard shoe Irish or tap... was this to make up for the lack of sound coming out of my mouth? I have also noticed that when I teach dance or speak in a dance class I never stammer, which is something I have always treasured.'

Tuning into your body

Modern life often distances us from our own bodies. Generally, we no longer use our own bodies as our primary form of transport, needing cars, trains or buses rather than walking. Advertising propaganda encourages us to wage war against ourselves – buying our way to some sort of impossible 'body beautiful' ideal.

Dance is the antidote to all of that. Dance shows us what we are capable of, especially if we are consistent in our effort. It shows us the beauty inherent in our bodies and helps us learn to trust them.

This chapter gives us a taste of all the ways dance is woven into our lives as humans, and as members of society. Dance is truly everywhere – both within us in our response to rhythm, creativity and beauty; it is part and parcel of our social and cultural practices, wherever we live in the world. We are dancing creatures, that is a given. The secret is to unlock the magic dance offers us so we can reach our full potential.

'I don't know why I dance. I only know I must.'
MARIE HALE,
founder of the original Ballet Florida

Carol Welsh, neuromuscular therapist, says

'Movement is a medicine for creating change in a person's physical,
emotional and mental states.'

Carol has been devoted to developmental movement since 1979. In
her unique movement training method, she pioneers her own
distinctive technique with an amalgam of principles from *Hanna
Somatics* ™, a form of mind-body training to address chronic
muscular pain.

She customises workshops for groups designed to meet the special
needs of dancers, athletes, sedentary workers, pregnant women and
seniors in the UK and USA.

Looking forward

I think we should all look at the ways dance is woven into life all
around us, and how it can equip us for the future, by helping us
develop skills and unlocking learning potential.

But what about now – the present moment? Let us look at how
dance can support us all in living well: whether that means feeling
happier or fitter, expressing ourselves, coping with change or dealing
with health conditions.

The feel-good effect of dance

We know that exercise triggers the brain to release endorphins, and
mood-enhancing neurotransmitters such as serotonin. It's why
exercise plays an important part in many mental health treatment
programmes. This in itself is a reason to incorporate more movement
into our lives: most of us instinctively know that we feel better after
getting moving, whether it's a swim, run or dancing around the
kitchen to music on our favourite radio station or playlist.

But it's not just about 'feeling better'. Dance can help people with
diagnosed mental health conditions and seems to be more effective
than other types of movement and exercise in doing so.

I understand that in a recent study, patients with anxiety-related disorders were assigned a place in a therapeutic class: either modern dance, exercise, music or maths. It was only those in the dance class who reported significantly reduced anxiety levels. *The Alchemy Project* in London developed a dance treatment for young adults suffering from psychosis. The participants were required to practice full-time over four weeks, learning dance routines in preparation for a performance in a professional theatre. The results were dramatic. On the Warwick-Edinburgh scale (a mental health and wellbeing scale widely used by researchers investigating mental health in populations), participants in the scheme saw a 7.9% boost in their mental well-being. This statistic compared with an average of 1.2% improvement through traditional NHS interventions.

Dance your troubles away

What's so special about dance compared with other forms of exercise? Miriam Berger, a dance professor at New York University suggests it's the relationship between movement and music. Dance activates our pleasure circuits, meaning we get an increased boost from dance compared with other physical activity.

Many people talk about 'coming out of themselves' when dancing.

Dance can be a way of expressing ourselves, which is particularly important if we're experiencing low mood, mental illness or find it hard to communicate in other ways. Academic Sarah Cook found dance a revitalising tool for coming to terms with her own depression, and her research has shown that to be true for others too. She says, drawing from her experience:

'Dance is a way of dealing with feelings and releasing them, rather than locking them in and going to the doctor with depression and anxiety.'

Gill Scard, ballet dancer, shares her experience to illustrate respect and perseverance in dancing troubles away. Her life has been enhanced by dance. She says;

'Dance still remains my first love, and so I attend a two-hour ballet class every week, and it is this class I would like to highlight. Our class is so much more than just learning the steps. We are of mixed abilities and talents. A couple of us have been trained professionally, some learned until they were teenagers, some only reached Grade 3 and a lot have no experience at all, but are committed to do their best even though it is a struggle at times. I admire this last group tremendously, it must be so frustrating to find something very difficult and unnatural, yet month on month they turn up and slowly improve. It may take them a term to get an enchainment right, but oh the joy! from us all when they do, far more of a victory than when I still pull out a double pirouette once in a while... by sheer chance I might add!

However, we are not just a group of winners aged from 30 to 70. We are a 'Family.' Eight years ago, I had a traumatic personal life-changing blow, and depression overcame my usual happy and energetic disposition. I fell into a pit that I could not crawl out of. The class rallied round and supported me. They listened, they swapped experiences and slowly the Joy of Dance returned, laughter and happiness dominate my life again at last. What I learned was that everyone in the class has experienced some sadness or difficulty in their life such as illness, unhappy marriages, challenging

children, low self-esteem, widowhood, elderly parent problems.
One of our loveliest dancers still comes to class (or to sit and watch) even
though she is battling palliative care at the moment. We encourage, we
support, we cry although we laugh far more than wipe away the tears.'

So, while dance isn't a cure-all, perseverance pays. It can certainly be a helpful ingredient to improving our mental health and sense of wellbeing.

Mindfulness and dance

Mindfulness, as a gateway to wellbeing, is becoming a more popular health concept. A large body of research suggests that mindfulness can help to reduce worry, aid sleep, and help us to connect better with others. Less well known is how dancing can help us adopt mindfulness practices in our lives, whether we are adults or children.

Mindfulness is the conscious act of paying attention to the present moment without making judgements. Often, 'ways in' to developing a mindfulness practice are focused on noticing your breath or sensations in your body. Dance offers a perfect opportunity for both these approaches, allowing us to focus our attention fully on what we are doing, how our body is moving and the breath that fuels our movement. Mindfulness, and all the benefits that accompany the practice are especially accessible to children, who may struggle with the idea of sitting still and focusing on their breath. This practice of fully focusing on the present moment is one of the key reasons why both dancers and mindfulness meditators talk about 'feeling alive'. This is perhaps another reason why dance is so good for our wellbeing – when it comes down to it, all of us want more of that 'feeling alive' vitality, rather than drifting through life on autopilot. The combination of music, our physical responses, and that sense we are truly living makes dance a powerful medicine for life's ills.

Dance as self-care

Life can pile pressures on all of us, from young to old. Children may worry about friendship dynamics and how well they are performing at school; while these may seem trivial concerns to adults, they are very real and troubling to the children experiencing them. Likewise, adults often find themselves in a hamster wheel of worry and stress, trying to keep life on track, balancing finances, commitments, and workloads.

It is no surprise then that looking after ourselves, we can fall to the bottom of the list, under the weight of other people's needs and expectations. Yet self-care is critical if we want to feel better. As the saying goes, 'You can't pour from an empty cup.'

Dance can be a powerful form of self-care. We have already

Former-pupil, Abi Murray, pictured here. Even though she is busy working in the music industry, including performing with her band Kavalla, she keeps time for dancing. This was a fabulous opportunity for her to dance alongside Darcey Bussell at The 2012 Olympics closing ceremony.

started to see the positive effects dance can have on your mind and body. There is also something important about making time for yourself and doing things that give you pleasure. The effects of this can be extraordinary for our wellbeing and sense of self.

My friend Kathi Doepfner tells how dance enhanced her life during a time of personal crisis:

'My husband developed a serious heart condition and later was on dialysis for the last five years of his life. Going to my dance classes was what helped

me keep my sanity. It was my escape from reality. For that hour and a half, I didn't have to think about my responsibilities at home. I know it helped me deal with my life at the time. I am forever grateful for all the support of my dancer friends developed over the years when I lived in New York. Dance was something I could completely devote my heart and mind to. Dance never let me down.'

The message is clear. When life feels busy and overwhelming, dance! Sign up for a local class if you can, or if not, put on some favourite music and let your body move. Don't make the mistake of thinking that dance, or looking after yourself, are frivolous or unimportant activities. They are quite the opposite.

Learning to love your body

People may assume that being positive about your body is at odds with the discipline of dance. And yes, for certain styles of dance at the professional level, lean body shapes prevail.

But dance is for *everybody*, and there is a style of dance for everybody. Dance doesn't have to be about pressure to look a certain way. At its heart dance is an expression of life and joy. It can be a demonstration of what our bodies are capable of if we treat them well. Dance shows us the power of setting goals and keeping going, and there is a real satisfaction in mastering steps that proved difficult just the previous week. That satisfaction in turn helps us to appreciate our bodies, developing strength and flexibility, and our ability to move at will.

Dance encourages us to focus on how we move, the shapes we make, and how we respond to the music – which is something we can all enjoy. It teaches us a growing appreciation for our bodies' abilities, which promotes a virtuous circle of boosting our self-esteem and making wise choices about how we treat ourselves.

Chapter 2
Dance lessons are life lessons

The quiet teacher

Dance is liberating, it's seen as an act of outward expression – often showy, often (not always) intended for an audience. Yet perhaps the most powerful aspects of dance are the lessons it teaches us without our realising it. We're not talking about mastering steps, or the finer points of technique here. We're talking about what dance can teach us about living well, about making the most of our lives and being a respectful and respected citizen.

Let me ask a question here...When you jotted down your notes in chapter one, did you consider what hidden life skills you or your children could uncover and learn from involvement in dance? Well, here's a chance to update your note from chapter 1.

- Creativity
- Perseverance
- Respect
- Confidence
- Responsibility
- Social Skills
- Focus
- Flexibility
- Gratitude

- Spatial awareness
- Social distancing awareness
- Leadership skills, looking at differing aspects
- Enjoying an activity with older/younger people

- Becoming a more knowledgeable spectator
- Musicality and appreciation of music
- Time management
- Pride of those around
- Inclusive movement
- Preparation for job interviews

Note all of the things in this list that you feel would help you or your child move forwards, then read on for more explanations and examples.

Of this list, which part would you be happy to accomplish? All aspects will become apparent as you read on.

When children or adults join a dance class for a number of weeks, months, or years, they see the progression in their dancing abilities. What might not be as obvious is the mastery dance helps us achieve in our lives.

For children, dance can be the introduction to skills that set them up for life. Teachers find dance is so powerful for children because it's all about movement – and movement is how we begin to make sense of the world, from babyhood onwards. For adults, dance can remind us of the hidden parts of ourselves, help us to unlearn limiting habits and beliefs and replace them with ones that lead us to happier, more fulfilling lives.

Dance brings so many of the unseen yet life-changing lessons if we open our eyes to them. In this chapter we touch on and give examples of seven of them, with the voices of professional and amateur dancers woven in to explain the impact dance has had on their lives.

Creativity

'To be creative means to be in love with life. You can be creative only if you love life enough that you want to enhance its beauty, you want to bring a little more music to it, a little more poetry to it, a little more dance to it.'
OSHO (1931 – 1990),
Indian mystic and founder of the Rajneesh movement.

Dance is important for creativity in two ways. Firstly, every dance movement is creative in itself. Even if you are following a teacher, you interpret the moves for yourself and pour your own self-expression into them. While the members of an ensemble are trained to dance in a similar way, we all bring our own essence to our

movement, feeling the music and the emotion our steps evoke.

If we choose to take part in freestyle dancing, whether it is informally at a party or with creative dance styles, we make choices about the shapes we create, how we interpret the music and the story we want to tell with our bodies, however simple. We play with rules, we use our instinct and create something entirely our own, in those moments.

Secondly, any form of dancing can help to boost creativity in all areas of life. Our brains respond to physical activity as well as an emotional release of pent-up feelings and energy. Researchers at the universities of York and Sheffield gave people a choice of how to respond to music: they could sit and listen, use an exercise bike and listen, or dance. Everyone was asked to do cognitive tasks before and after the experiments. All the dancers showed more improvement in their problem-solving and creative thinking skills, as well as reporting being in a better mood.

So, if you're looking to bring more creativity into your life – get dancing, whether it's to a tune on the radio or at a weekly class!

Perseverance

As with most things in life, you are unlikely to be brilliant when you first start, and you're unlikely to get better unless you keep going. Dance is a clear example of this. Regular practice is vital, not only for mastering steps, but for improving your strength and stamina. After a while you look back on the routines or steps you found tricky a few weeks before and feel that sense of satisfaction that they're safely under your belt. Because dance is physical and outwardly expressive, it is easier for us to witness the effects of perseverance than, say, with reading or writing skills.

The combination of movement, music and our innate urge to perform means dance is often a first love or obsession for many children. This makes it a perfect first lesson in perseverance, overcoming difficulties and learning from mistakes. Such learning is vital to other hobbies, academic studies and working life.

Gylly Rutherford, a former senior executive in British Airways (BA) says:

> *'The training I received as a dancer taught me to never give up! That has followed me through life, especially in BA where my role was to take care of heads of state, royalty, VIPs etc., most of whom were highly demanding. Perseverance was paramount!'*

In her book, *Hope in a Ballet Shoe,* Michaela DePrince tells her story about perseverence personified.

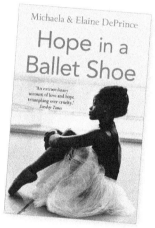

> *' I believe... because I am the little girl who dreamed of being a ballerina and now dances Black Swan Pas de Deux with Dance Theatre of Harlem'*

Focus

Closely related to perseverance is focus. Concentration is becoming a lost art in our constantly switched-on and fast-moving world. But focus is critical in any dance environment; whether you're dancing solo, with a partner or in a group dance. It requires you to be aware of what your body is doing now, what's coming up, how the rest of the space in the room (or on stage) is being used. Spatial awareness appears to be lost to many, judging by the bustle of busy streets and train stations.

So dance is an excellent training ground for developing the ability to focus. It is only possible to do so when you have a clear goal. In an academic environment, or a broader social setting, the goal may be more abstract – to understand fractions, or to demonstrate kindness, for example.

With dance, children are able to see clearly what's expected of them in class from the teacher's demonstration, and are given the time to watch, try and practise. They have the space to focus, and they can see first-hand the benefits of concentrating on their goal, both in the long and short term.

Sue Barbour applying her ballet training into walking on stilts:

'My parents were in show business and believed that ballet was the basis for all dance so sent me to audition and apply for a scholarship to Elmhurst Ballet School then in Camberley, Surrey. I won the scholarship and was at Elmhurst for seven years. At 14 years old I decided that I wanted to act and sing as well as dance in my career. My first job was as the 'Fairy' in pantomime (I was 14 years old). I did a dance on pointe and the older dancers objected because the producers would only pay for my pointe shoes and provided them with flat ballet shoes. Later, when I decided to join my parent's act, I danced on stilts. My ballet training helped me enormously as we used to do high kicks on the stilts and balance was essential. Dancing on stilts enabled me to tour the world and earn a living! I am now a House Parent at Elmhurst and dance is still important to me as it helps me form a strong link with the students I look after.'

Respect

From the formal révérence at the end of a ballet class, in which the students bow/curtsey to the teacher and accompanist, to the respect dance teaches us for our bodies, respect is woven through dance practices.

Révérence

The poses of these young students are part of a movement called révérence. The curtsy for girls and bow for boys are a simple form of what is usually a longer and more elaborate movement. In class, the révérence is traditionally the last step done before the class ends. On stage, too, this is the final thing the dancer does. As a performance finishes and the audience expresses its appreciation with applause, the dancer, in turn, acknowledges the audience with the révérence.

Ballet is a beautiful, exciting, and wonderful art to learn about, to perform, or to enjoy watching!

We will learn more about the role of dance in education later in the book, but this student's experience from the Dancing Classrooms School programme in Florida shows us the magic of respect: for dance, for others, for ourselves. It is recounted by her dance teacher:

'When this young lady came to school, she felt she needed to prove herself and make sure everyone knew she was strong and would fight. The girl didn't want to join the ballroom dancing program, but participation wasn't optional.'

By her fourth lesson the teacher commented:

'she carries herself differently, she speaks differently, she is kind, she is respectful. Her mother can't believe what she sees. It's amazing.'

Dance requires us to listen to our teacher, fellow students, and ourselves, to respect the steps and the slow progression through increasingly difficult techniques. It is through paying respect to the music, the process of learning, the wisdom of the teacher and ourselves that we gradually master dancing. Dance without respect is chaos.

Confidence

Dance builds confidence, because it asks us to take charge of our bodies, improving our relationship with ourselves. Confidence only ever comes through taking action, through *'feeling the fear and doing it anyway'* to quote the classic self-help book *Feel the Fear and Do it Anyway* by Susan Jeffers. Dancing as a hobby is a gentle outlet to experiment with this – the stakes are low. You might feel as though others will laugh at you if you get a dance move wrong, but the reality of that happening in a beginner class is low indeed, when everyone is in the same boat.

It is also a valuable outlet for people who don't have a chance to shine in other aspects of their lives. Lisa Patrick, a parent, describes how dance has helped her daughter to build confidence. She says:

'I am able to tell the story of my daughter who, when writing this, was nine years old. She started dancing at age three when she was very shy and would give no eye contact to new people she met ...however she always would say a few words with a smile to her dance teacher.

In school at age four she became socially mute only saying the odd word if a teacher persisted, even with myself, her mum, working in the classroom. She did however make friends and chat to those that attended her dance classes ...

When she was seven, the diagnosis was given that she had dyslexia, slow processing as well as discalculus. Every day she struggled, but now at age nine within the walls of the dance studio, or on the stage, she transforms into a confident well-spoken child with so many true, lovely friends. The knowledge, determination and focus she is gaining from attending these dance lessons, where the teachers understand her quirky ways and appreciate her for just being her, have truly transformed our lives.'

So dance is there for all of us – to show us that there is more than one way to be successful, and all the things we can do if we are prepared to give it a go. It can demonstrate to us the people we can become if we take the risk and dance our way to exemplify confidence.

Responsibility
Daniel Negrin, (1917 – 2008) an American modern dancer, choreographer, teacher, and author, profoundly said:

'Ultimately, we resort to one authority, one critic, ourselves. Laying claim to that prerogative and that responsibility gives us the right to consider ourselves as artists. By allowing anyone else final authority in our choices and actions, we disallow that right. An artist is a person who is ultimately responsible for his/her action.'

This isn't only true of the professional artists and dancers. It's the case for all of us and dance is a very tangible example of how we are responsible for our own decisions: how to move, when to practice, whether to bother showing up. We make our choices, and we live the consequences of those choices. Dance shows us very clearly that taking responsibility for ourselves brings its own rewards.

Leadership

Dancing offers practical opportunities to learn about leadership, whether it's through trying your hand at choreography, taking the lead in partner dancing, or teaching others.

What makes a good leader in any situation? There are hundreds of answers to this question, but according to the Center for Creative Leadership, in Greensboro, North Carolina, USA, it comes down to four key skills, which are well demonstrated in the dance environment.

Self-awareness: understanding your strengths and weaknesses. There is no hiding from your body on the dance floor, which makes dance an excellent teacher in self-awareness – we cannot help but learn more about ourselves.

Communication: a leader needs to be clear about what they want to achieve and effective in communicating to their followers. Dance provides an opportunity to do this, whether it's through the cues you give your partner, the explanation you give your students or the musical interpretation you share when choreographing.

Influence: you can't be a leader without followers. Dance enables you to share your vision with others and help them work with you to achieve it. It involves working together, not leaving people behind and ensuring everyone feels the level of passion and commitment required to make the dance a success.

Learning agility: as leaders and as dancers we are never finished. There is always more to learn, more to develop, more to understand. Just as dance develops our perseverance, it develops our openness to learning, and teaches us to walk the tightrope between pride and humility.

Social skills
Dance brings us together. At a dance class we meet new friends and peers, whether we are adults or children. For some, these classes can be a lifeline, a place we can truly feel at home.
Dance classes have sets of social rules – they teach us how to give and take, the importance of listening, and taking part. Dance classes give us the opportunity to test new ideas, to be aware of others and our impact on them, and the value of working together to create something greater than the whole. Even a solo performance requires choreography, teaching and musical accompaniment. Dance recognises the value of working together.

Whether our dancing life begins at three, 30 or 73, dance can always offer new insight about how to conduct ourselves well. These foundational concepts of creativity, perseverance, focus, respect, confidence, responsibility, leadership, and sociability are the building blocks for life. They enable us to pursue our dreams, bring others with us and keep going in the face of difficulties.

Gena Walker, owner of Gena's Dance Academy, Peel, Isle of Man, provides an insight into the impact of dance on her life:

'To be honest, I would be lost in life without dance. I possibly couldn't imagine what else I would fill my days with - it's all I know and I feel

extremely privileged to have been brought up with this disciplined art form that is full of beauty. From training to become a dance teacher to now owning and running a busy dance school on the Isle of Man, I would encourage everyone of all different ages and backgrounds to try out the wonder of dance and the positive effects it has on the mind, body and soul. My dance school is a haven for all ages and I think it is extremely important for these different groups to gain interaction with each other, whether it be socialising in between classes, younger students watching and looking up to the senior dancers or working all together to produce our biannual showcase.'

Dancers from Gena's Dance Academy

Dr Peter Lovatt (Doctor Dance) of the University of Hertfordshire, UK, explains:

'Dancing stimulates us physically and emotionally while there are also cognitive and social elements to it. For many people, dancing prompts an emotional release – often that's uncomplicated happiness, while for some it can make them cry. It's cathartic – a letting go of pent-up emotions.'

Doctor Dance is *The Dance Cure: The surprising secret to being smarter, stronger, happier,* published in the UK by Short Books in April 2020.

Fitness expert Matt Roots, writes:

'Dancing also improves spatial awareness, as well as raising the heart rate and causing a release of feel-good endorphins into the bloodstream. One more benefit is that it helps reduce levels of cortisol – a stress hormone. That's another reason why it makes you feel happy and more relaxed.'

The story of Cheryl Carty, board member of The Manatee School for The Arts, Florida, USA and founder of their dance school is inspiring.

Cheryl blossomed in a dance environment and won a full scholarship to North Carolina School of the Arts. She has since established dance studios and is a powerful advocate for the work at Manatee, which infuses the arts in all academic programmes, enabling students to access multiple intelligences and makes use of a variety of learning styles.

In Cheryl's own childhood, dance was a way into stability and education. She says:

My home life was unbalanced, erratic, and sometimes, terrifying. However, my mother enrolled me in ballet class, and I found my lifeline.

There are people who dream to dance or want to dance or simply need to dance. I am someone who needs to dance.

My mother loved to dance and had some talent when she was 15. She was asked to join a ballet troupe travelling through their city, but her father said absolutely not, 'No daughter of mine is going to be one of those kinds of girls.' She was sent to business college instead.

Much later when she married, she opened a dance studio for a little while before my parents divorced, which in the 1960s was taboo.

In her grief and low spirits, my mother and I danced in the living room, and I copied her waving arms, slowly then wildly, as we danced to a poem about tree branches that blow in the wind.

My parents divorced when I was six and that was only complicated because my mother, by then, had mental depressions several times a year. In those days they treated this mental ailment with pills referred to as 'uppers and downers.' This was medicine for disaster.

In ballet class there was structure. There was peaceful, classical music. There was exercise, sweat, and work. I liked the work. I needed the music. I needed to dance! I needed to know a reality that was uplifting, and I found that peace in the world of ballet. Swans, love, romance, and 'happily ever after' was somehow the fairy tale that ignited my imagination and survival instincts. Luckily, I had talent and excellent teachers in our local dance studio in Clearwater, Florida. I was poor and these teachers gave me a scholarship to dance. They also gave me the freedom to grow and become who I would become as a dancer and a person. Their generosity, my work scholarship, and my Christian Science Sunday school classes gave me the buoyancy to ride the turbulent waves of my life as an 8–15-year-old while my mother's episodes grew darker and a diagnosis of schizophrenia was soon to be determined.

At 15, I was offered a full scholarship to North Carolina School of the Arts (NCSA). I had to ask my mother if I could leave home and join the school. Since we were poor, this opportunity was a blessing. She knew how much she had loved ballet when she was 15, and she knew regret. She let me go, although I know she needed me. I would find out later how much I needed her. My mother had courage and gave me a great gift of freedom. And in my gratitude, I have continued to pay it forward in as many ways as I can.

I have had a ballet studio, and I have two sons both of whom were raised in dance.

I do feel that I have 'paid dance forward' to my children, like my mother paid it to me. The arts is a language of abstract to concrete expression, and there is nothing like it. It starts as a language of the heart then develops in mind and body. For me it was a therapy for Soul, and I cannot live without its pulse.

Since I currently teach at Manatee School for the Arts (MSA) in

Sarasota, Florida and am a founding board member for this 20-year-old Public Charter School, I am proud to say that the dance department has grown significantly. Where once there was 6th grade dance, tap and jazz, now there are 3-4 levels of Tap, Jazz, Ballet, Modern, Ballroom, Irish, Pointe, and Hip Hop pre-professional classes. MSA has eight dance studios and thirteen full time dance faculty.

At MSA I have started a school ballet company and have been able to enrich the education of young dancers to remain after school and apply their ballet skills with new story and choreography.
I see the students who dream to dance, I watch and train the dancers who want to dance. But most importantly, I look for dancers who need to dance, for I recognize their struggle to emerge whole. I encourage the ones who must dance. Those dance students have a persistence of heart, soul, and skill, unpatrolled. Perhaps, like me, they need to defy gravity, find life-balance, and experience reality in a new world of music and aesthetics – a world their individual talents help create. At the very least, all dancers of dreams, wants, and needs, express themselves in ways that teach them physical strength, co-ordination of large and small motor skills, appreciation of all kinds of music (especially classical), understanding of body language, expression of movement as communication, artistic expressions, and all the pre-planning and rehearsing work ethics that come from a passion. And if they work hard and are lucky like me, the dancer who NEEDS dance will have a lifetime paid professional career.

My career included travelling with a ballet company from Carnegie Hall, called American Chamber Ballet, as well as spending many years' tap dancing with the Rockettes (at Radio City Music Hall) and a brief moment with New York City Jazz Company (Fancy Dancer – John Medrios/Gene Aguire). From there I was in many musicals, became the dance Captain, then the assistant choreographer, and then the choreographer. These days I am now a director/choreographer, and have I had the pleasure to work with many students in many different musicals such as Annie, Shout, The Sound of Music, Cabaret, Chicago, Crazy for You, Oliver, Camelot, Brigadoon, Music Man, to name a few. I hope this book and these stories by my inspiring friend, Sue, will *inspire anyone to dance, to dream, and to find out what they need. Here's to staying buoyant and balanced in life. For me, ballet, was that significant turning point.'*

Cheryl Carty is the embodiment of how dance education changes lives. And from being supported by her childhood dance teachers to studying at NCSA, she has spent more than two decades educating the next generation of dancers.

Roy Castle was a dancer from childhood, he grew up into a multi talented performer. His wife and widow Fiona, who has also supported We Can Dance Charity, shared this photo of Roy as a child, just starting out in Yorkshire, and tells this story.

One story was that he was in the Guinness World Records Book for doing a million taps in just under 24 hours, also for doing 24 taps a second (which I never believed!!) but the reason he took up tap dancing as a small child was that he was quite a puny lad and he said that his knees were the thickest part of his legs!

His mother sent him for tap dancing lessons, because she said......in her very Yorkshire accent - " 'appen they'll thicken yer legs oup lad" In other words, perhaps it will help you get better shaped legs!

" In 1991 Professor Donnelly, world renowned surgeon who carried out the first removal of a lung cancer by keyhole surgery, which brought international publicity, put together his ideas for an international research facility in Liverpool. He went to Roy Castle to ask for his help. His response was magnificent and, although he was dying of lung cancer, agreed to a 'Tour of Hope' by special train around the UK which raised over £1m in three days during July 1994 for the charity ".

At each train stop Roy and his wife Fiona would emerge to entertain the thousands of people who had turned out to hail his talent and bravery, and to donate to the cause.

Professor Donnelly said "His contribution cannot be exaggerated. He was with us for only eight months but in that time, he captured the hearts of the nation. He is still very fondly remembered. After Roy died, the trustees agreed that we should put his name to the charity and so we became the Roy Castle Lung Cancer Foundation".

"This is not for me – this is for our children and our children's children."
ROY CASTLE

Even through death, this wonderful entertainer, dancer and gentleman is still impacting the success of the charity in:-
The Roy Castle Lung Cancer Tapathon.

https://www.facebook.com/roycastlelungcancer/
photos/a.466467663652/10155515177043653/?type=3

Rhee Gold is an American dance industry pioneer and icon who founded the Dance Life Retreat Center. Teachers and studio owners flock to his retreats, seminars, keynote speeches, and conferences to gain fresh perspectives. His columns, inspirational messages, and opinions are shared all over the world. He says:

For me
dance is life!

It's a gift that becomes entranced in
the soul. Those of us who feel this
way have trouble describing it to those
who don't, but I think of it like this:
there's a point when the movement and
the music grab hold of you and fill
you so completely that you become more
than a body moving through space:
you become art!

RHEE GOLD

Chapter 3

Our dancing world

Dance is universal: in this chapter we explore why dance is such a powerful force in the world, and see how dance can enrich our lives, whatever our personal views of our own dancing abilities.

Dance all over the world

Dance has been part of human society since the earliest civilisations. the oldest cave paintings show scenes of communal drinking and dancing. It's likely that the earliest forms of dance accompanied rituals, which is still true today, especially in indigenous cultures.

But dance evolved to serve many purposes all over the world today.

Celebrate

People dance to celebrate either in traditional folk celebrations, such as Maypole dancing in England, Germany to celebrate spring and fertility, Bon Odori, a dance is performed in July during the festival of Obon in Japan to welcome the spirits of the dead. At family occasions such as weddings and even funerals, dance is present when people gather.

Party

There are dozens of folk dances across each continent (except perhaps Antarctica!) From the Italian tarantella or

Indian bhangra to the Brazilian samba. These dances are part of everyday culture, taking place at various social occasions, with dancers having little formal training, and simply learning from others in their communities and joining in.

I remember visiting Brittany in 1990 with my daughter Joy and being part of such an occasion. We joined a group of locals who were going to be dancing in the local village hall. Joy and I entered the hall to find a myriad of people ranging from young children to seniors. Grannies and Grandpas took great pleasure in sharing their knowledge with the less experienced. We joined in when everybody rose to their feet and were warmly welcomed. The movement flowed between the bodies and young, old, male and female had enormous fun. We learned new dance steps and realised that within that framework great family unity was evident and generally friendships formed. We came away very happy.

Healing Power

From specific medical rituals such as the Vimbuza healing dance performed by the Tumbuka people in northern Malawi, to the development of dance/movement therapy (DMT) in the USA, dance is recognised as a way to heal from illness and boost wellbeing. Movement and music are a powerful combination.

Dance in everyday life

It is perhaps easy to think of dance as a quaint practice that happens mostly in traditional cultures or children's classes these days. But dance still plays an important part in modern life. While it may seem that many traditional rituals have been lost, we still find ourselves turning to dance for parties and celebrations: consider the role of the 'first dance' in many wedding celebrations for example. Or how, when people want to relax and let their hair down, it's the nightclub dance floors that often call. Most birthday parties feature music and dancing at some point.

Music and dancing draw us all in. As humans, we are creative beings. Dance is a form of play, of expression, it is a release. And despite our often stubborn resistance, it always attracts us. Think about the popularity of TV shows such as *Strictly Come Dancing* (UK) or '*Dancing with the Stars*' (USA). These shows have taken the ratings by storm because of our compulsion to see music and movement together – with the added celebrity ingredients of course! And, just for fun, monitor the ads next time you're watching TV – you'll be surprised at how many of them feature dancing. Dance sells because we are attracted to it.

A form of social glue

Martha Graham the iconic American choreographer and modern dancer, (1894 – 1991) once said:

'Dance is the hidden language of the soul.'

She was right. Dance crosses all sorts of barriers: age, ability, religion, language, culture, in ways that the spoken and written word simply can't.

It's no surprise that many wedding customs feature the bride's family joining the groom's in dance pairs, once the happy couple have had their first dance, as a symbolism of the families uniting.

The power of dance has wider implications. In New York City, 'Dance to Unite' is a non-profit organisation established to celebrate differences and promote cultural diversity, by providing free after school dance classes. Its founder, Galit Adani, says:

'Dance is not the focus. It is a vehicle. The main goal is that at the end of the year students will view differences in a more positive way.'

It is this wider purpose of dance that we are interested in. Dance isn't simply about fancy, impressive movement, though it's certainly inspiring to see what the human body is capable of with dedicated training. It's about bringing people together, finding new ways to express ourselves and opening up the world.

It's not only those in the dance world who believe in the broader power and purpose of dance. Research has found that dancing helps increase connection and brings people together. Working with a hundred children, the researchers found that those children performing similar dance moves felt closer to each other. The finding raises interesting questions about how we can make use of dance to build bridges with each other as well as celebrate our differences.

Dance is for everyone

Importantly, dance is inclusive. Whatever your abilities, you have the right and the freedom to dance. This makes dance a fantastic tool and hobby for all of us, including people with additional needs. Some activities might be out of reach for people with physical mobility issues, sensory processing disorders or other neurodivergent conditions. But dance is not.

Dance enables all of us to join in, to work together, to become more aware of our bodies and how we interact with others. This was the primary reason I set up *'We Can Dance'* (www.wecandance.co.uk) a

charity providing dance lessons across the north of England for children in schools with special educational needs. A percentage of the profits from this book will go to further the work of We Can Dance. Instructors now teach regularly in more than 17 schools across County Durham, Cleveland and North Yorkshire. Amazingly, they were able to continue lessons throughout the Covid-19 pandemic. This was achieved through generous grants.

A UK street dance group Autism With Attitude from Hillingdon U K, demonstrated the power of dance when they became the first special needs group to reach the United Dance Organisation's European Championship in 2018, using their position to educate people about autism and what people with autism are potentially capable of.

https://www.optionsautism.co.uk

Another very compelling read is this article by Louis Kavouras. It epitomises much of my belief. I'm sure you will find it fascinating.

What I Learned in Dance Class by Louis Kavouras.

'When I was eighteen during a difficult phone conversation, I had to tell my parents that I was giving up my full scholarship at one of the best engineering schools in the country to instead pursue a major in dance. Of course, my parents were supportive and cared about the desires in my heart, but their voices also revealed the sound of disappointment and uncertainty, that maybe it would be difficult for their son to have a financially stable career as a dancer and an artist. For my parents, like many educated caring parents, they thought that the dance classes that were consuming so much of my time and passion, were socially an incredible outlet, and gave me a great place to express myself, discover myself, and create beautiful art. What they didn't realise, and maybe I didn't either at the time, is that I was learning so very much more in these dance classes.

In dance class, I was learning:

- *Organisation*
- *Problem Solving and Memory*
- *Being Calm Under Pressure*
- *Communication and Expression*
- *Leadership and Teamwork*
- *Individuality*
- *Balance of Mind, Body And Spirit*
- *Decision Making Skills*
- *Confidence and Positive Self-Image*
- *Commitment to Practice*
- *Diligence and Commitment to a Team*
- *Productivity and Risk Taking*
- *Honesty/Integrity*
- *Motivation/Initiative*
- *Ability to Build Relationships*
- *Flexibility and Adaptability*
- *Standards for Success*
- *Self-Awareness*
- *Understanding of Space/Time/Energy*
- *Numeracy, Accounting, and Structure*
- *How to Please/Market to An Audience*
- *Innovation/Passion/Performance*

And I was not only learning the concepts of these profound areas, I was learning how to implement them in myself and in the world around me. I graduated with an undergraduate and graduate degree in dance, performed in New York with a professional dance company, travelled the world performing and choreographing, became a professor of dance and chair of one of the best university dance departments, and went on to write and teach the world about all that dance is. And what I realise now is that the above list of skills that I learned in dance class, well....these are the exact skills and traits that top employers in this nation are looking for in their top executives. And these are also perhaps the traits we find in most successful individuals. And underneath all of the pliés, tendus, contractions, dance phrases, and dance compositions, in dance class there was this other level of profound learning that was going on. People sometimes wonder why do some individuals develop such a strong and unwavering passion for dance. I feel that often there is only one thing that makes a dancer. They are special individuals who sense and feel movement in a special and profound way. And when they discover dance, for the rest of their lives, THEY HAVE TO DANCE. When someone begins a career in dance, there is no set pathway to follow. Each will individually find their own way and construct their own successful and fulfilling life. And the skills that we learn as dancers, allow us to be entrepreneurial and successful in worlds that extend far beyond the dance studio and the theatre. There are an infinite amount of job opportunities for those who are trained as dancers. This is what I wish I knew during that tough phone conversation. Dancers like most artists learn to be fearless, and constantly face the unknown and the opportunity for something new, something different, and something exciting. When a painter encounters the blank canvas, the writer the empty page, the actor the play script, the filmmaker the empty storyboard, the composer the empty musical staff, or when the dancer steps into an empty studio space, they are stepping into a realm of infinite possibility. There is no better or more exciting place to be.'

Louis Kavouras is the Chair of the Department of Dance at the University of Nevada, Las Vegas (UNLV). Trained as a modern dancer, he performs with the Erick Hawkins Dance Company in New York and is curator of the Erick Hawkins Dance Collection/Hawkins West Institute at UNLV. He teaches dance, choreographs, lectures and writes about dance and its significance.

Louis gave me permission to include this article in this book. I am so grateful to him. We have never met but have come to the same conclusions about the amazing skills that dance teaches.

Cassie Cooper, a former pupil of mine and now a parent of dance students, shares her view of how dance affected her:

'I danced only briefly when I was a child but I always remember how it made me feel which is why when I have had children of my own I wanted them to experience the pleasure of dance. My son and daughter dance regularly in all styles: tap, modern, ballet and hip hop. When they danced together for their first show I was so very proud of them both. Seeing your children dance in a professional production brings so many emotions to a parent, I especially will be feeling grateful that they get the chance to take part and be part of a company. My son will, I hope, always feel confident that just because 'he is a boy' he will still be able to feel positive about the world of dancing and be able to be true to himself. It is wonderful seeing his pure enjoyment of working with a teacher who really helps him be the best he can be. All a parent asks is for their child to have opportunities and be happy. Dance offers so many versatile skills: rhythm, coordination, 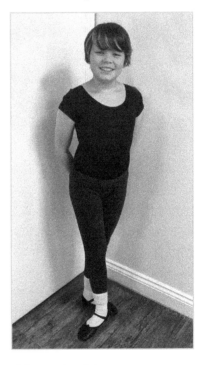 *exercise are only a few..the most important to me are self-discipline, imagination and a coping strategy for life.'*

Soon you will learn more about dance with differing abilities. However, read these quotes below, and you will be convinced that all children should have the opportunity to dance.

Dancewear Central, a renowned Dancewear shop in Blackpool, commissioned an article for their website and have kindly agreed to share it.

6 Things children learn in dance class that aren't dancing

www.dancewearcentral.co.uk / August 16th, 2017

'Behind every young dancer is a parent or two whose responsibility it is to write cheques for dance classes, buy ballet, tap or jazz shoes and leotards, sew costumes, and play taxi driver to and from lessons. But it's actually about so much more than that.

When parents from all over the UK recently responded to a Facebook page which shared their appreciation and love for dance, the overwhelming message was that, behind all the hard work, late nights and mountains of ballet shoes, parents gladly do it all so their children receive all the benefits of dance class – and it's not just about the technical dance skills. **Debbi Fullilove, who owns Yorkshire-based Dance Stars**

UK, shared her thoughts: *'Encouraging children to dance is much more than just the physical element, exercise and getting children away from an indoor environment. Children have a thirst to learn and develop, and dance – from musical theatre to street dance – is a great way of helping them grow and come out of their shell. 'In a day and age where many children are scared of how they may be accepted, there is nothing more rewarding as a dance teacher than seeing them flourish.'*

With this in mind, dance experts across the country were consulted and we discovered the biggest benefits of dancing, and why there's more to classes than meets the eye.

1. Patience

Children aren't the most patient creatures in the world – any parent can attest to that. And the younger they are the less patient they seem to be! Throw an exciting dance class into the mix – where they get to run around and burn off that excess energy – and it suddenly becomes harder to keep them still.

Dancers, both professional and amateur, constantly have to wait their turn, whether they're moving across a stage, freestyling or demonstrating an individual move. Knowing when it's your turn to move and then to be still and quiet while another has their go is a skill we use long into adulthood.

The sooner children learn when to take their turn, the sooner they'll learn to interact better with others. Conflicts will be reduced and their social skills will blossom.

2. Confidence

As children learn to dance, hone their technique and take a performance from start to finish, their confidence grows. Add that to gaining a better sense of their bodies and feeling more comfortable in their own skin, and their self-esteem will skyrocket.

They'll learn how to express themselves, which is really what dancing is all about, and it's what separates it from other physical activities. It gives kids a physical outlet for their emotions, a place to be themselves, and they're encouraged to be proud of that.

Johanna Hadley, teacher at _Janet Lomas School of Dancing_, Bury, Lancashire UK says that increased confidence through dance is something children will take with them into later life:

'I myself have seen students who were once shy and withdrawn grow in confidence – in later years they have blossomed into beautiful dancers, happy and willing to perform in front of large audiences.

'A student who has regularly walked into a dance examination room or performed on stage will be unfazed by the university admissions process, job interviews and public speaking. Dance teaches the ability to present oneself in an assured and professional manner, and the weekly attendance of these classes demonstrates both dedication and commitment.'

3. The way the body works

Kids are curious creatures, and they love to learn about the world around them. Put them in a class where their body does wonderful things like moving to music, and they'll be eager to learn more about how they actually do it. And this can stand them in good stead for later life.

Naomi Wallen, owner of _Dance Matters_, a community dance school in Bassingbourn, Royston UK says that learning about the body through dance can influence children's future path:

'When you know how a body jumps, you can jump higher, farther, quicker. Introducing the concepts of anatomy when the children are young will allow them to build upon this foundation in the future. They will learn that there is more to their bodies than what they see in the mirror.

'If a child becomes intrigued by their body, they may develop a life path for themselves. I know former dancers who are now doctors, nurses, midwives, physiotherapists and pharmacists. Additionally, if a child learns how amazing their body is, their relationship with their body can be a positive one. Body image is a difficult part of the lives of children and young adults – any opportunity to embrace the brilliance of our bodies is worth the work.'

4. Improved social skills

Dancing isn't all about the individual – even in more solo disciplines such as ballet or tap. As part of their class, children will be asked to communicate and cooperate with their fellow students, both in pairs and in groups. For shy children, in particular, dancing can be a really big help and encourage them to come out of their shell as they talk to others and make new friends.

Debbi Fullilove believes that people often underestimate that dance can take soft skills straight back to basics: 'Dance is about encouraging children to have fun, while increasing basic core skills that can benefit them in future life. This includes verbal communication through socialising with their peers, listening skills, and also encouraging them to take ideas and develop them.'

5. Friendship

Improved social skills are just one branch of dance, and dancing often requires children to work together. Making friends comes easily to children – they seem to be able to talk to anyone and at any time! So place them in a room full of similarly aged children where their only task is to move to music, and they're bound to interact and before you know it they've formed a bond.

Naomi Wallen believes that friendship is one of the biggest benefits that children take out of the dance studio: 'They learn how to be friends with people who aren't the same as them. Our classes are mixed gender. Some have a range of ages, and some dancers have learning disabilities. The children discover how community is a gorgeous thing and how role models can be found in unexpected places. Learning how to socialise with others from an early stage is a vital part of a child's cognitive development. Dance brings together children from a variety of backgrounds and personalities, creating an environment outside of the child's comfort zone. Children are encouraged to learn to adapt, connect and communicate in new ways. They learn to build trust and effective relationships.'

6. A healthy body

Children weren't made to sit still, but watching television or playing video games can turn from an occasional treat into a daily habit. Dancing gets them out of the house or moving to music from home on Zoom on a regular basis, and while you may not be looking for your kids to lose weight, it helps to keep their heart, and brain, healthy.

Giving children the confidence and encouragement to move while they're young will give them a taste for physical activity that they carry with them into later life. Whether they become a professional dancer or not, they might continue with amateur classes as an adult or migrate to a completely different sport – it doesn't matter as long as they move.

Chapter 4

A dance education

To me, education is a leading out of what is already there in the pupil's soul.
Muriel Spark (1918 - 2006), a Scottish novelist

What does education mean to you? Is it about learning a body of established knowledge and passing tests? Is it about learning about the world and yourself? Is it about becoming a responsible citizen? Education means different things to different people. Whatever your definition, it may surprise you to learn that dance teaches discipline and embraces the spirit of learning.

To recount, dance can play a vital role in education: helping children embrace learning, prepare for working life and understand themselves better. How dancing helps the brain, and how the transferable skills of dancing melds invisibly into great learning skills.

The dancing flame

For many, education represents being 'made to learn'. Pupils turn up to school and try to take on board the subjects on offer. This approach suits some children, but not all. For those left cold by the lessons on offer, dance stimulates an appetite for learning.

Letting children immerse themselves in doing something they enjoy elevates the potential of learning.

Children are more likely to apply themselves to a subject when they are genuinely interested, and for many children, dance ticks that box from an early age.

Dance should be part of every young person's education since it provides creative, healthy and stimulating experiences. If every young person has the opportunity to experience dance, it offers huge potential for developing creativity and innovation across the curriculum.

Since 2014 children are entitled to study dance as a subject as part of the Australian Curriculum. Dr Katrina Rank, who developed the programme in Victoria, Australia, is on record as saying:

'My interest in the curriculum is for it's creative and critical potential and in the ways it engages the whole student kinaesthetically, kinetically, spatially, visually, inter and intra-personality.'

Dame Darcey Bussell, DBE, has formulated a children's dance fitness programme called Diverse Dance Mix (DDMIX) just for this purpose. She explains:

'The aim of DDMIX is to get people moving without being intimidated by the word 'dance' or the technicality of the steps, but instead to give a full body workout that is such fun that you don't even notice that you are exercising. With the vast number of dance styles around the world to choose from, no one will ever get bored!
I have a passion for dance-based fitness and believe the best way of getting fit is by doing something you enjoy.
By participating in dance, you can achieve your goals by not looking upon exercise as a chore. At DDMIX we love group exercise classes with non-correctional instruction that are fun and all inclusive'

Dancer Jessica Hoffeldt writes:

'Dance taught me how amazing life can be when you're truly passionate about something. Having a passion for something gives you the motivation to keep at it and push on even when things get tough.'

Ballet performance at Elmhurst Ballet School, UK: The Mandarin gives a Party 1960

Learning for its own sake

Compared with many forms of exercise that children engage in, dance is non-competitive. Yes, there may be the urge to do better than classmates in exams, and there may occasionally be competition for roles in a performance, but for the most part, dance students find they are competing with themselves. They are challenged to learn something new, to have a go, then practise, receive instruction and support, and they get better.

This pattern of learning is called intrinsic motivation, and it is incredibly powerful. When people are naturally motivated, they do things for their own sake, because they find them personally rewarding. Compare this approach to the reasons many of us, young and old, do at school or work: for rewards – whether that's good grades, privileges, money or praise. This type of external reward system creates extrinsic motivation. And it can be useful. But the problem with extrinsic motivation is once the reward goes away, quite often, so does the behaviour, or the motivation to do your best. How many of us would work for free or do homework for fun? Some of us are lucky enough to do work we enjoy – we are the happy few. But, many dancers, young or old, keep dancing, regardless of any reward.

Once we have a taste of the internal satisfaction intrinsic motivation brings, we want more! And so, dancing creates learners – people with that little flame inside them, hungry to learn more, for its own sake, and for the joy of it. With that comes the lesson that life isn't always a bed of roses and if you want to get to the next stage, learn the new piece, you have to put the work in. But when you have the flame inside you, it's so much easier to keep going, for you have that sense of the bigger picture and the rewards that come with learning.

Movement and learning

Psychologists and educationalists now agree there are three main preferences: visually (through what you see around you), auditory (through what you hear) and kinesthetic (through movement and touch). While teachers often try to incorporate plenty of moving around for children at the kindergarten stage, that mode of learning is frequently neglected as academic studies continue, with older children and adults learning mainly through reading or listening to lectures.

For optimal learning. all three elements need to be incorporated. Dance is an exemplary way to learn these three traits. Students get to move their bodies in response to watching the teacher, and hearing instruction and feeling the music.

For students who respond best to kinesthetic learning, dance can open fresh insights. In 2010 a primary school in County Durham, UK – then an area of high economic and social deprivation - gained funding to teach a class of seven-year-olds through dance and movement for a month. The pupils participated in a process known as 'dance and learning inspired education'.

While the results weren't fully quantifiable, the teachers, dancers and children all agreed the outcome was astounding. The pupils demonstrated levels of engagement and creativity not seen before. They were able to share what they'd learned with researchers several weeks after the experiment had finished.

Dance for the long term
A unique programme, Dance - The Next Generation (DNG) in Sarasota, Florida, USA, puts the discipline of dance at the heart of education. The programme, primarily focuses on children at risk of dropping out of school. Through free dance tuition and supervision for homework, dance is the backbone to these children to develop the discipline and self-respect to stick with their studies and make a tangible difference in their lives. The more academically minded students are encouraged to apply for scholarships entitling them to free university education - a life-changing opportunity for any young

person. One graduate of the programme puts it like this:

'Along with such simple blessings as graceful posture and uncanny balance, I learned to keep pushing myself when things became difficult. From a young age I was shown what it felt like to commit to a long-term goal and see it through to the end.'

The late Sue Robinson, English Ballet teacher extraordinaire, recognised that all children can benefit from dance classes and should have the opportunity to dance, whether continuing with a dance career or not. Obviously, not all of Susan Robinson's pupils went on to become professional dancers or teachers.

'I always say, if you never dance a step as a professional, it is [Dance Lessons] not wasted, because you've been with like-minded girls and boys, you come through puberty in a very healthy way and just get on with life. And I think the camaraderie that the girls have, the friendship they've spawned, they've kept. I like that about them, because they're nice human beings and it really matters not whether they danced or not. With us here they did dance, and they danced with joy.'

Elmhurst School friends with Robert Parker Artistic Director of Elmhurst Ballet School.
Photo left to right:
Anna du Boisson, Sue Robinson, Robert Parker, Sue Hewgill Peterson, Annik Coatalen Heal

Susan Robinson personified the joy of teaching.

Dance unlocks passion and potential

It is dangerous to assume we all learn in the same way. Potential can be lost if we are blind to it. In his powerful book '*The Element: How Finding Your Passion Changes Everything*', educationalist Sir Ken Robinson recounts the tale of Dame Gillian Lynne, a dancer, choreographer, producer and director with over 60 Broadway productions to her name. In the 1930s when Gillian was at school, her parents were advised that she had learning difficulties because she couldn't sit still and wasn't completing her work. The school recommended seeking professional help.

Luckily, the psychologist who saw Gillian was perceptive. He put the radio on and saw how she moved to the music. Rather than recommending remedial studies, he advised Gillian's parents to enrol her in dance classes, where she thrived. Imagine instead if Gillian had been diagnosed with ADHD (Attention deficit hyperactivity disorder), or been told she had to adapt to a non-moving learning environment, we wouldn't have the remarkable choreography of Cats or Phantom of the Opera for starters. What a miserable, unfulfilled life Gillian would have led in comparison to all she has achieved. Dance unlocked everything for her.

The same was true for Cheryl Carty, board member of The Manatee School for The Arts (MSA), and founder of their dance programme in the school. It is a Charter school. These schools in the United States, which are primary or secondary education institutions, do not charge fees to pupils who take state-mandated exams. Some Charter schools provide a specialised curriculum (for example in arts, mathematics, or vocational training). Charter schools are attended by choice. The MSA focuses on the Arts and has some two thousand students, eight studios and three theatres.

In a face-to-face interview with Dr. Bill Jones, Founder and Principal of Manatee School of the Arts, was asked 'How do you measure impact of the arts?'

'A lot of it for me is looking at the dance classes the kids take. I watch them and go to as many productions as I can. I like to watch the growth of students. When you see all of that happening, you get the feeling you're okay. It is very hard to quantify well-being and the affective domain of objectives for example. You look at behaviour, like value systems, this is the only way to see improved behaviour in the school.'

Lighting up the brain

Whether we have a kinesthetic preference or not, movement helps all of us learn. Researcher Eric Jenson, a proponent of this learning, says in his book '*Teaching with the Brain in Mind*':

'Simple biology supports the link between movement and learning. Our brains need a good flow of oxygen to work effectively. Movement enriches this flow and fuels the brain with neurotrophins, which increase the number of connections between neurons. In short, movement helps our brains work more effectively. Jenny Seham, a dancer, choreographer, and clinical psychologist observed the positive social and academic changes in children who dance. Their grades improved, as did their self-discipline and sense of purpose in life.

Similar improvements in grades have been reported by participants in the USA 'Dancing Classrooms' programme, which provides free dancing lessons to school children. One teacher from an elementary school in the US Virgin Islands reported that by the second year of her school's participation in the programme, reading and maths scores in her class had gone from failing to an 83% pass rate.

As Sir Ken Robinson puts it, quite simply,

> 'The body is a form of transport for the head.'

The future of work

In this fast-changing world, no-one knows quite what the future of work will look like. Jobs that children will be competing for don't exist yet. This pace of change requires a new approach to education – one that doesn't simply tell us what we need to know. Instead we need education that gives us the skills to respond to change and apply learning ourselves.

The global management consultancy firm, McKinsey & Company investigated scenarios for the future of work in its 2017 report *'Jobs lost, jobs gained: What the future of work will mean for jobs, skills and wages,'* It projects that future workers will be in far more need of social and emotional skills such as collaboration, and higher cognitive skills such as creativity and problem-solving. Automation is likely to take care of much of the rest.

Where does dance fit with this? We have seen how incorporating dance into our lives can help develop critical social, emotional and cognitive skills. Dance offers us an opportunity to see the world differently, to take risks, to try things for ourselves, to develop social connections, to solve problems through creativity and perseverance – all themes that are likely to feature strongly in later 21st century work life. Dance provides a toolkit that extends far beyond its own subject.

Sir Ken Robinson tackles these issues head on in his article and lecture *'Why Dance Is Just As Important as Maths in School.'*

He argues that dance cultivates the skills needed for employment and life. Rather than restrict the school curriculum to narrow subject areas monitored by output, dance and other arts subjects can create a rich culture for learning, applicable to all areas of life and future development. He says,

> *'We teach to create well-rounded citizens who can apply the skills, knowledge and experience from being involved in the arts to their careers and lives.'*

Dance enables us to deepen our skills and knowledge, including all the cultural, historical, musical and spatial elements. This in itself is important, as dance through the ages has been entwined in what it is to be human – learning about dance helps us understand the world better. It is a route into understanding music, history, geography, physiology and psychology, among many other subjects.

Alan Foster has a Professional Dancers Postgraduate Teaching Certificate. He says:

'That is the reason I am telling you my story; thanks to my Royal Academy of Dance educational qualification I am now working as a dance teacher in China. Dance has taken me around the world, shown me different cultures and given me so much pleasure, and now I get to pass on my experience. Dance of any kind is so good for children and provides such valuable learning experiences. Persistence, collaboration, reflection, creativity, problem solving, all of these things are enhanced through dance. But dance is not only for the young. I have been inspired by the Silver Swans,* and by the many older dancers I have seen on social media who are still keen to learn and reap the rewards, both physical and mental, that are to be gained through dance. In the future, as well as teaching children and young adults,

I hope to put on classes and workshops for older people who may have always wanted to dance but never got the chance. If you have the passion, it is never too late to learn.'

Silver Swans has been specially devised by the Royal Academy of Dance for older learners to help improve mobility, posture, coordination, and energy levels.

Silver Swans class; Sudbury, Suffolk

Far more than that, dance unlocks the capacity for much broader learning. As you can see from Alan's story, it can ignite a passion for learning. It improves our ability to process new information and gives us the opportunity to develop skills. It truly is an education in every sense of the word.

Consider the other end of the spectrum now. Let us think about the early years too. Here is the story of two amazing ladies who have developed a special programme for little ones from six months up to six years old.

It is the leading dance programme for babies, preschoolers and young children winning numerous awards. It brings such joy and pride to the children and their grown ups enjoying the magic of dance classes in a fun, relaxed and supportive class environment. Mother and daughter team, Claire O'Connor and Barbara Peters BEM FRAD, are immensely passionate about Babyballet and have worked tirelessly since 1999 to make it into the award-winning reputable concept it is today. There are now more than 100 franchised and licensed schools teaching over 25,000 children every week in the UK, Australia, New Zealand and Singapore.

Claire says,

'I wanted our children to experience something different and so we invented a magical world of dance filled with characters, colour, music and fun – a world where every child gets the chance to be valued and shine.'

The syllabus has been developed for children from six months to six years and it is noncompetitive. From 2022 A separate SEND (special educational needs and disabilities) programme was devised. The scope is remarkable.

Dancing with a robot

I was fascinted by the article in Dance Magazine. My curiosity has been piqued by Ms Denton and Dr Moore. Read below quotes from articles about both these innovative women.

'Living in space means relearning, and, in some cases, redefining, how the body moves. Astronauts must develop entirely new ways of choreographing their space.'

C. Adeene Denton February 8th, 2022 *Dance Magazine*

'The way astronauts live, work and play may not seem like dance in the traditional sense—it lacks both the performative trapping and any familiar movement vocabulary we might seek to recognize—but when we consider who they are, and where they live, the legacy of the International Space Station (ISS) comes much closer to a 20-year-long, site-specific performance piece than I expected when I began to study it. It uses a specially developed movement framework to captivate its audience. In this case, the audience is the rest of humanity, and the astronauts are the performers, tasked with building a vision of low-Earth orbit as a place where the lack of gravity liberates us, where the idea of what movement, and, thus, dance, can be is completely transformed.'

'If I manage to make my way to space, I won't be the first person to make art out of motion up there. But I'll get something better—the chance to build on a long and proud legacy of low-gravity movement. It's a fascinating new realm for dance, one that's been fun for me to watch astronauts explore. Maybe one day, I'll get the chance to join in.'

I thought that there was one profession that could not be replaced by robots, professional dancing. Until I was privilaged to meet Dr Merritt Moore, in 2020 on board the Queen Mary on our Atlantic crossing to USA. She has choreographed and danced with a robot! Education has certainly been pivotal in her diverse and successful career. I have included here two articles. She recounts her early career and also about her Robot, named Baryshnibot", dancing experience to Tess Thomas, editor of Assembly, a digital newsletter and publication of the Malala Fund.*

Dr Merritt Moore, has been described as the "quantum ballerina'", because she couldn't choose between a career as a ballerina or a career as a physicist. So she decided to do both. While pursuing degrees in quantum physics at Harvard University and the University of Oxford, she also performed with companies like the Boston Ballet, English National Ballet and London Contemporary Ballet Theatre. Tess says of Dr Moore:

'She knows her path is unconventional, but,it seems that she couldn't imagine her life any other way. She finds that dancing helps unlock her creativity as a scientist and approaching ballet from an analytical perspective helps push herself physically. Merritt wants to show girls that science and the arts aren't mutually exclusive — and that you don't have to be defined by just one interest. Dr Moore believes that gratitude and appreciation are crucial for excelling in any craft. As I do. Having a disparate career/passion helps create appreciation because it keeps things in perspective and makes one really appreciate what a privilege it is to have a chance to do either. She says that for instance when she is exhausted in the dance studio, there is nothing more that she would want to do than to curl up with a physics book in a library, and when she is cooped up reading all day, it keeps her hungry to get back into the dance studio and try new movement. This is such an amazing insight. She wants to give advice to anyone pursuing their passions, she suggests Newton's 3rd law of motion: "For every action, there is equal and opposite reaction" because it is a great motto for life.'

Something else that I really believe dance teaches us, and Dr Moore agrees, is learning to bounce back from failure really fast. She says that she auditioned so many times and was rejected often that it doesn't disturb her anymore. In fact, she knows that every time she

* *Co-founded by student and Nobel Laureate Malala Yousafzai, Malala Fund works to create a world where all girls can learn and lead.*

puts herself out there, she is improving and getting closer to succeeding. So far it has included professional ballet companies, virtual reality film projects and dancing with robots.

At the beginning of the Covid-19 pandemic, Dr Moore didn't realise that her only dance partner for the foreseeable future would be a cobot. This didn't stop her from turning the world of dance on its head and creating beautiful and unique performances with her new robot partner.

Dr Moore says:

"There are so many rigid stereotypes of what a dancer or a scientist should be, and this can be really damaging for both disciplines. For scientists and engineers, creativity is key in finding new solutions to problems. For dancers, the ability to be technical and analytical can take your practice to the next level"

Her pas de deux with a UR10e cobot ,named "Baryshnibot" by her Instagram followers, defies expectations and is a remarkable composition of grace and poise between man and machine.

The unusual partnership began in Oslo where Dr Merritt was performing Swan Lake and La Bayadere with the Norwegian National Opera and Ballet. Through mutual friends she met Silje Gabrielsen, senior designer and co-founder of Hiro Futures, a human-robot interaction start-up based in the Norwegian capital. Gabrielsen says:

"We research artificial social skills in robotics. One of our focus areas is how we foster better collaboration between humans and robots. Today's robots are still lacking several skills to properly collaborate in non-industrial settings. Instead of simply using a screen or additional hardware to communicate and interact with humans, we want to use a more intuitive communication system; body language."

Dr Moore was one of 12 selected astronaut candidates to undergo rigorous selection process on the BBC Two show *"Astronauts: Do you have what it takes?"* under the guidance of Commander Chris

Hadfield and continues to pursue that dream. She says:

"My dream of becoming an astronaut is one of the big reasons I work now with robots. I feel like it is an expertise that will be highly needed in the future of space exploration and that it will make my application to National Aeronautics and Space Administration (NASA) even stronger."

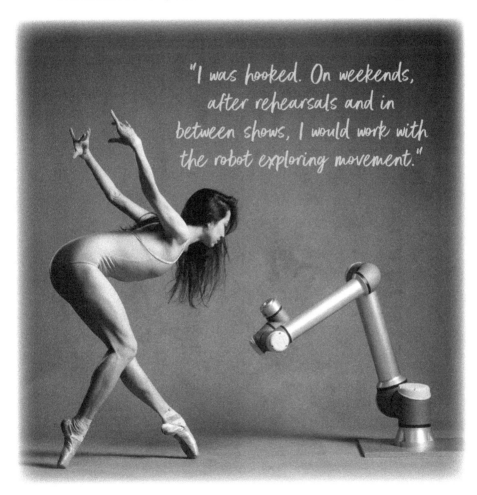

"I was hooked. On weekends, after rehearsals and in between shows, I would work with the robot exploring movement."

So, Dancing in Space next I suppose!! Let us watch out for that with anticipation. I wonder which dancer will join her in space. Could it be you or a dancer you know? Or maybe she will dance with a robot in space.

Chapter 5

Dance and ageing

Dance can help us to build bridges across cultures, and communities. For children and adults alike, dance can be a social lifeline, a joy in life, a way to gain new friends with shared interests. A way for perhaps for three generations to become involved together.

Here is an article that shares some of these ideas.

Dancing with Granny?

"Dancing with the elderly for 15 minutes could improve memory and overall health"

Elderly dancing

Israeli doctors found out that dancing for 15 minutes a day lifts the spirits of the elderly and strengthens a family's bond, according to the *Daily Mail*. It can also bridge relationships across the generations. A Daily Mail report in 2020 by Edwin Diaz, looked at a study by Israeli doctors who found that dancing for 15 minutes a day lifts spirits of the elderly, improves their memory and overall health and strengthens a family's bond.

The research paper, *Free-Form Dance as an Alternative Interaction*, for adult grandchildren and their grandparents, found that *Dance Movement Therapy* (DMT) empowered the grandmothers and their grandchildren who danced with them. The aim was to see if the 'joint dancing of an adult grandchild with his or her grandparent would contribute to improving the relationship and to familiarity between them, and will improve the older person's physical, social, and mental status.'

How dance can change the world in a few steps

In the study, granddaughters copied their grandmothers, being encouraged to expand their dance moves, make eye contact, touch, and engage in playfulness. In turn, the granddaughters empowered their grandmothers and advised them to rest if they needed to do so. It 'created a change in the grandmother's state of mind: positive memories and feelings appeared, as did uplifted spirits,' according to the article.

The granddaughters were the dance movement therapists in the study. The researchers found that the perspective of the grandchildren on old age changed during the experiment. It also reduced anxiety and depression levels had fallen in the elderly.

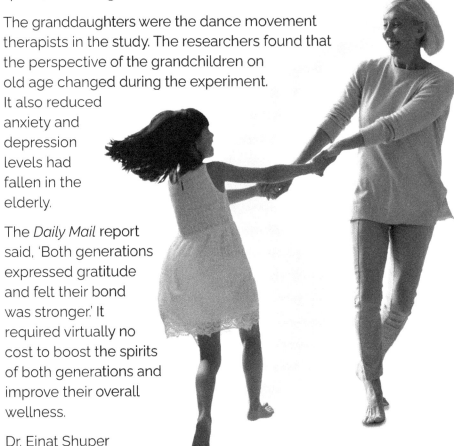

The *Daily Mail* report said, 'Both generations expressed gratitude and felt their bond was stronger.' It required virtually no cost to boost the spirits of both generations and improve their overall wellness.

Dr. Einat Shuper Engelhard, one of the

authors of the Israeli study, says:

"Increase of the proportion of elderly in the population, along with the increase in the age group of adult grandchildren, necessitates creativity and innovation in providing diverse resources and support."

She added that the bond will only increase if the activity is between the grandchild and its own grandparent. Dancing together will also alert grandchildren about the support needed as their grandparent ages. Making dancing a habit can also make the elderly stronger and family ties tighter.

Dr. Engelhard adds:

'The unique framework of the meeting promoted physical activity even when the body was fatigued and weak and in circumstances where the grandparent was not accustomed to participating in other physical activities. It creates new memories and introduces opportunities for the pair to know each other more.'

The study, first published by Imperial College London, also discovered that dancing can 'Help to improve treatment for patients with chronic dizziness.' Research has shown that 30% of people older than 65 years experience dizziness in some form, according to Annals of Family Medicine.

Psychology Today also recommends incorporating 'some type of dance at least once a week' to maximise brain function. In an article, *The Cognitive Benefits of Movement Reduction: Evidence from Dance Marking*, it said practising routines using marking, which means means working through a routine in the mind or in a simple fashion, reduces mental strain needed to perfect movements.

For the elderly, this is good news. Reducing mental strain will help seniors achieve good mental health. The World Health Organisation observes: *'Many older adults are at risk of developing mental disorders, neurological disorders or substance use problems as well as other health conditions such as diabetes, hearing loss, and osteoarthritis.'* Introducing dance into their daily routine, even for just 15 minutes, will make a huge difference.

Sharing the joy and love of movement or perhaps grandparents joining in dancing with adult grandchildren, say at a cèilidh or in a regular class can be very beneficial to both of them. Encouraging mums or dads to take a class at the same studio as their offspring is another inspiring idea. When I was Executive Director of a Performing Arts Centre in North Carolina, we offered a father and daughter session. It was very well received.

Modern life has created a 'loneliness epidemic'. In 2018, the UK developed a 'loneliness strategy', recognising the importance of dance and other social activities for people's wellbeing. In 2020 dance classes were made available by doctor's prescription!

Karin Fulcher, my school friend who now lives in Canada, writes how she sees dance as her prescription for life:

'While surgery on my feet at the age of 12 precluded a career as a dancer, ballet has given me a basis for all my activities throughout my life. I have always done some form of movement whether aerobics, Zumba, step classes, swimming, skiing, ballet, or yoga and I believe

this has contributed to a strong skeletal base, and ease of movement. Now in my seventies, I am still supple and agile and attend four or five yoga or exercise classes weekly. Occasionally people will still comment on my deportment which is encouraging!!'

Dance doesn't discriminate by the usual socio-economic factors. In a dance class you can make friends with people from all neighbourhoods, ages, and walks of life. For children, their 'dance friends' can often have staying power beyond their school friends, as the friendship is based on shared interests. For adults, the connections we form can be very special. As DeeDee Wilde, who was a dancer in Pan's People and danced on the 60s famous TV show Top of the Pops, tells us from her own experiences:

'I have been dancing for 52 plus years and am now in my 70s and I'm still dancing! After my family and friends, it is the most important thing in my life and always has been.

'I trained as a classical dancer first but soon realised I was not to be a prima ballerina! This held me in good stead because in December 1966, myself and two other dancers formed Pan's People. We went on to become one of the most famous dance groups in England. This was mostly due to our weekly appearances on Top of The Pops, a highly popular music show on BBC One.

'Although it wasn't classical ballet, I still feel very proud of what we achieved, my parents' money wasn't wasted! I spent 10 years with the group and met many famous people from the Beatles to Michael Jackson.

'I also performed for four months at The Royal Opera House in Covent Garden. I danced the part of Erda in Das Rheingold. This is a part sung by a soprano, but I went down in history as the first person to dance the role rather than sing it!

'Dancing is one of the most wonderful art forms; it is totally expressive, all-consuming and very uplifting. In my latter years I have

been teaching like-minded women the joys of moving to music.

'This has been very beneficial to them and of course me. For some of them dance has changed their life and I feel proud to think that through my classes they have improved their lifestyle, made friends, felt healthier and found a passion in dance.

'I have no intention of giving up dancing in the near future but spend my time careering around the West Country doing festivals, talks and demonstrations on how it is never too late to dance no matter what age you are!'

Dance and older people

The Centre for Policy on Ageing (CPA), based in London, says in a report that only around 17 per cent of women aged 64-75 and 20 per cent of men get enough physical exercise, and this statistic falls to fewer than 10 per cent for over 75-year olds. Dance therefore is a fantastic way for older people to build exercise into their lives, as it can combine aerobic and low-resistance exercise with the emotional benefits of attending a weekly social commitment.

'Dancing makes you feel alive, almost like you're young again
... I don't know anything else that can have that effect on you
... maybe it's the music, the people
... I don't know.'
Young@Heart participant, 2009

Young@Heart is an entertainment group featuring a chorus of senior citizens, with an average age of 80, from Massachusetts, USA. The group cover songs by Jimi Hendrix, Coldplay, Sonic Youth, and other musicians. A British documentary about the group was directed by Stephen Walker.

I understand from a BUPA (British United Provident Association) report, in research which was carried out for Bupa by the Centre for Policy on Ageing (CPA), that the older population in many parts of the world is growing rapidly and, at the same time, it is becoming more diverse. Recent projections suggest that, in England and Wales alone, by 2026 there will be more than 10 million people aged 65 and over, of whom 1.3 million will be from black and minority ethnic backgrounds. As people age they tend to adopt an increasingly sedentary lifestyle but there is widespread and compelling evidence that increased levels of physical activity will improve both the longevity and the health of older people. The BUPA report also reviewed the international evidence for the health benefits of dancing for older people. Exercise programmes for older people commonly experience high drop-out rates. Dance, on the other hand, is an enjoyable and sociable form of exercise where participants report very high levels of motivation.

Dance is also increasingly catching the public imagination. In 2010 more than 10 million viewers tuned in to watch episodes of the BBC1 TV programme Strictly Come Dancing and it continues to delight the nation. The Strictly format has spread to more than 50 countries. This increased interest in dance provides an opportunity to offer dance sessions for older people in community centres, care homes, village halls and hospitals across any country. Local dance projects for older people have been set up in many parts of the UK. Similar programmes of dance, including ethnic dance, for older people, have been adopted worldwide including recreational dance in Australia. There are a number of benefits to dance for older people: dance is inclusive and one of the principles of community dance for older people is that anyone and everyone can take part; dance can be tailored to match the physical capabilities of an older person and dance can also reflect the cultural diversity of the older population. In addition, dance is a social activity and, as such, can benefit both the physical health of older people and promote a sense of well-being and social inclusion.

Dance helps to develop aerobic power, muscle strength, endurance and balance and flexibility, as well as having numerous other health benefits, such as helping to prevent falls. A pioneering programme in the UK, *Dance to Health* was created and is delivered by *Aesop Arts and Society*. *Aesop* is a charity that uses the arts to help solve a challenge society faces. The *Dance to Health* programme uses dance to help people improve or maintain their strength and balance. This is important to ensure participants continue to get the most out of life. It also reduces pressure on the NHS (National Health Service).

Dance to Health has combined dance with physiotherapy to offer classes focused on preventing falls, and there is time for a chat over a cup of tea after the session. Older people are more at risk of experiencing loneliness than the general population, so opportunities to come together with others are particularly important. Aesop's nationwide community dance programme for people aged over 55 are led by professional dance artistes from leading dance companies who have been fully trained and qualified in falls prevention exercise methods. I understand their online sessions are available to anyone.

I have been lucky enough to be immersed in dance all my life, and credit dancing with keeping me feeling young enough to take on challenging full-time employment in my seventies.

We are now looking at dance for us. For someone like me, dance has always been part of my life, and I am extraordinarily grateful for that. Since my working life started in earnest I have been fully employed. As well as that, I have had such wonderful experiences through life and people tell me that it is keeping me young! Enough to consider taking on a full-time job in my seventy second year. Life is full of exciting opportunities, and we must step forward and take them. So, I suggest, if you feel inspired to dance or to encourage others to, and this applies to young folk as well, you must go ahead. I can give examples of ladies and gentlemen who in their senior years are still excelling in the dance field.

Here are examples of how dance can help with overall wellbeing. Whether starting out late in life or as a young child it is proven that general life skills can be learned through studying and having fun and achieving goals through the medium of dance.

First we look at two ladies who have definitely achieved a fabulous lifestyle through dance.

Maureen Dye (Mo to everyone) who formed an all-adult ballet programme in around 2000 called *Dancing thru the Years*. It is still going strong, working out of a Bradenton ballet studio in Florida.

Mo is not afraid to say she is over 80, she still teaches ballet to adults in Florida USA. She still demonstrates and is interested in all aspects of her pupil's life and learning.

Whilst we were doing research for this book, Mo wrote:

'DANCING changed my life! It changed who I might have been ... I wish I could find exactly the words to describe just how and to what extent. Just double or triple the impact of every description that I have tried to give, and you might come close to how .... because of MY DAD'S INSISTENCE AND PERSEVERANCE in getting me almost daily to my DANCING STUDIO won for me... continued confidence, respect and joy throughout my entire life, and as I age.... growing respect and admiration from so many people.
HOW LUCKY I AM !!!'

The second is Barbara Peters.

Any dancer would be delighted to pass a top ballet exam. Barbara Peters, in her eighties and a widow from Halifax, UK, passed her RAD (Royal Academy of Dance) Grade 7 ballet exam at the age of 80. She has appeared on national television and felt full of vim and vigour. She says:

'I was told that I had passed with merit the grade seven exam and have become the country's oldest ballet dancer. I am thrilled, it was the best gift I received.'

When you do that at 80 – and pirouette into the record books as the country's oldest ballet dancer – it is all the sweeter. That is the birthday present that

Barbara Peters starting out on her long dancing career.

great-grandmother received. Subsequently Barbara passed her Grade 8 with similar marks. What an amazing achievement!

Barbara is pictured here with her daughter, Halifax-born entrepreneur Claire O'Connor, who together established the dance franchise Babyballet.

Barbara began dancing as soon as she could walk at the age of two, took her first dance exam at nine and has devoted her life to ballet ever since. In 2022 Barbara was made a Fellow of the RAD (FRAD) and appeared on the new year honours list 2022, receiving the British Empire Medal (BEM) for her dedication and work with ballet and dance.

In her career she has worked as an examiner for the RAD for many years and has rubbed shoulders with Dame Margot Fonteyn and Dame Darcey Bussell. Barbara says:

'Ballet has kept me fit and raising my leg a metre high to place my foot on the barre was easy. I also held my leg straight out front and side at a 90 degree angle for a few seconds'.

'I can only do two pirouettes on the trot now but still do cartwheels, though I haven't done the splits for the past ten years'.

For more on Barbara's story visit:

http://www.dailymail.co.uk/femail/article-5268707/Britains-oldest-ballet-dancer-passes-elite-exam-aged-80.html#ixzz54ZnhlLe8

Another example is Eileen Kramer, an amazing lady who is still dancing and performing in Sydney, Australia where she was born in 1914. She is a dancer and choreographer. Eileen joined the

Bodenwieser Ballet—Australia's first modern dance company—in 1939 and then spent many years living in India, Europe and America before returning to Sydney in 2014. I have read that she lives at Thurlow Castle, Sydney, 'A home for the potentially homeless'. She has collaborated on many projects since then. At 103 years of age, Eileen Kramer continues to create: she performs, designs costumes, draws and writes on a daily basis.

She was quoted in *Huffington Post* as saying....

'Everything happens at 100, everything changes'. She says that she has received more attention than usual since she entered triple digits, an age she describes as magical. However, more impressive than the fact that she dances at all is how she dances, with soft and sinuous gestures that move like billowing folds of fabric.

A fellow dancer friend, Anya McKee, says 'She is such a beautiful creative spirit and a really physical body still at more than 100 years old. So the idea that you need to stop dancing in your 30s or your 40s and you have to get everything done before then, it's just gone, it's not true.'

To find out more about the amazing lady Eileen Kramer look on YouTube, also look up on Wikipedia or Huffington post.co.uk

https://www.bing.com/videos/search?q=ballet+dancer+103+years+old&&view=detail&mid=41FA3CD7C345B8A594B241FA3CD7C345B8A594B2&&FORM=VDRVRV

Finis Jhung Who was born in 1937, lives and works in America. Eighty-four years old in December 2021, Jhung feels stronger than ever during and after teaching three ballet and a stretch class weekly — before, during, and after the Covid-19 shutdown. Able to show all barre exercises, waltz and balancé, pirouette and steps en l'air without muscle cramps or discomfort

during or after. Able to walk up six flights (the elevator to his apartment is frequently broken.) Credits his well-being to daily meditation, total right hip replacement in 2017, daily stretches and self-massage, eating wisely, and working with people who love ballet. His pictorial memoir *Ballet for Life* available on Amazon.

Another gentleman of note is Sir Peter Wright, CBE (born 1926). He is a British ballet teacher, choreographer, director, and former professional dancer. He worked as a choreographer and as the artistic director of *Birmingham Royal Ballet*, the classical ballet company based in Birmingham, England, upon retiring from the company in July 1999, age 73 he was bestowed with the honorary title of Director Laureate of the company.

In this photo are Sir Peter Wright with principal Dancer Mathias Dingman and First Soloist Miki Mizutani

This photo is of The Sarasota Ballet's Director Iain Webb, Assistant Director Margaret Barbieri, designer Dick Bird and Sir Peter with dancers from The Sarasota Ballet before the 2015 revival of **Summertide**.

In 2021 The Sarasota Ballet Company, Sarasota, Florida presented Sir Peter Wright's magnificent **Giselle** and sparkling **Summertide** to celebrate the choreographer's 95th birthday.

Here we highlight Debbie McGee (born October 1958) she has had dance and movement flowing through her life and illustrious career. She is an English television, radio and stage performer who is best known as the assistant and widow of magician Paul Daniels. She tells me-

"You don't have to be a good dancer. It is your own expression of the music. Dance keeps your body toned, it keeps your heart and brain healthy, it frees your mind and brings you joy. Dance makes you feel young. Which is why I LOVE IT"

Learn about her on her very interesting website: **www.debbiemcgee.co.uk**

She is President of The Cup of Kindness Grand Order of Lady Ratlings and Honorary Vice President The Magic Circle London.

Chapter 6

Dance and health conditions

Here is a great article from Richard Powers. He has been teaching historic and contemporary social dance for more than 40 years. He leads workshops around the world and is a full-time instructor at Stanford University's Dance Division, Stanford, California, USA. He shows us how dancing frequently offers wonderful, enhanced lifestyle opportunities. Most of this chapter is dedicated to this article.

Use It or Lose It: Dancing Makes You Smarter, Longer.
Richard Powers
July 30, 2010, Copyright © 2010, 2015 Richard Powers

For centuries, dance manuals and other writings have lauded the health benefits of dancing, usually as physical exercise. More recently we've seen research on further health benefits of dancing, such as stress reduction and increased serotonin level, with its sense of well-being. Most recently we've heard of another benefit: frequent dancing apparently makes us smarter.

A major study has added to the growing evidence that stimulating one's mind by dancing can ward off Alzheimer's disease and other dementia, much as physical exercise can keep the body fit. Dancing also increases cognitive acuity at all ages. You may have heard about the New England Journal of Medicine report on the effects of recreational activities on mental acuity in ageing. Here it is in a nutshell.

The 21-year study of senior citizens, 75 and older, was led by the Albert Einstein College of Medicine in New York City, funded by the National Institute on Aging, and published in the New England Journal of Medicine. Their method for objectively measuring mental acuity in aging was to monitor rates of dementia, including Alzheimer's disease.

The study wanted to see if any physical or cognitive recreational activities influenced mental acuity. They discovered that some activities had a significant beneficial effect. Other activities had none.

They studied cognitive activities such as reading books, writing for pleasure, doing crossword puzzles, playing cards and playing musical instruments. And they studied physical activities like playing tennis or golf, swimming, bicycling, dancing, walking for exercise and doing housework.

One of the surprises of the study was that almost none of the physical activities appeared to offer any protection against dementia. There can be cardiovascular benefits of course, but the focus of this study was the mind.

There was one important exception: the only physical activity to offer protection against dementia was frequent dancing.

Reading - 35% reduced risk of dementia
Bicycling and swimming - 0%
Doing crossword puzzles at least four days a week - 47%

Playing golf - 0%
Dancing frequently - 76%.
That was the greatest risk reduction of any activity studied, cognitive or physical.

Neuroplasticity

What could cause these significant cognitive benefits? In this study, neurologist Dr. Robert Katzman proposed, that these persons are more resistant to the effects of dementia as a result of having greater cognitive reserve and increased complexity of neuronal synapses. Like education, participation in mentally engaging activities lowers the risk of dementia by improving these neural qualities.

Information from Wikipedia on Neuroplasticity, also known as neural plasticity, or brain plasticity. It explains that it is the ability of neural networks in the brain to change through growth and reorganisation. These changes range from individual neuron pathways making new connections, to systematic adjustments like cortical remapping. Examples of neuroplasticity include circuit and network changes that result from learning a new ability, environmental influences, practice, and psychological stress.

As Harvard Medical School psychiatrist, Dr. Joseph Coyle, explains in an accompanying commentary:

'The cerebral cortex and hippocampus, which are critical to these activities, are remarkably plastic, and they rewire themselves based upon their use.'

Our brain constantly rewires its neural pathways, as needed. If it doesn't need to, then it won't.

Aging and memory

When brain cells die and synapses weaken with aging, our nouns go first, like names of people, because there's only one neural pathway connecting to that stored information. If the single neural connection to that name fades, we lose access to it. As people age, some of them learn to parallel process, to come up with synonyms to go around these roadblocks.

The key here is Dr. Katzman's emphasis on the complexity of our neuronal synapses. He says:

> 'More is better. Do whatever you can to create new neural paths. The opposite of this is taking the same old well-worn path over and over again, with habitual patterns of thinking and living.'

He mentions that when he was studying the creative process as a graduate student at Stanford, he came across the perfect analogy to this:

> 'The more stepping-stones there are across the creek, the easier it is to cross in your own style.'

The focus of that aphorism was creative thinking, to find as many alternative paths as possible to a creative solution. But as we age, parallel processing becomes more critical. Now it's no longer a matter of style, it's a matter of survival — getting across the creek at all. Randomly dying brain cells are like steppingstones being removed one by one. Those who had only one well-worn path of stones are completely blocked when some are removed. But those who spent their lives trying different mental routes each time, creating a myriad of possible paths, still have several paths left.

As the study shows, we need to keep as many of those paths active as we can, while also generating new paths, to maintain the complexity of our neuronal connections.

In other words: **Intelligence — use it or lose it.**

Intelligence

What exactly do we mean by 'intelligence'?

You'll probably agree that intelligence isn't just a numerical measurement, with a number of 100 plus or minus assigned to it. But what is it?

To answer this question, we go back to the most elemental questions possible. Why do animals have a brain? To survive? No, plants don't have a brain and they survive. To live longer? No, many trees outlive us.

As neuroscience educator Robert Sylwester notes, mobility is central to everything that is cognitive, whether it is physical motion or the mental movement of information. Plants have to endure whatever comes along, including predators eating them. Animals, on the other hand, can travel to seek food, shelter, mates, and to move away from unfavourable conditions. Since we can move, we need a cognitive system that can comprehend sensory input and intelligently make choices.

Semantics will differ for each of us, but according to many, if the stimulus-response relationship of a situation is automatic, we don't think of the response as requiring our intelligence. We don't use the word 'intelligent' to describe a banana slug, even though it has a rudimentary brain. But when the brain evaluates several viable responses and chooses one (a real choice, not just following habits), the cognitive process is considered to be intelligent.

As Jean Piaget 1896-1980. a Swiss psychologist known for his work on child development, put it,

'intelligence is what we use when we don't already know what to do'.

Why dancing?

Let's ask two questions:

• **Why is dancing better than other activities for improving mental capabilities?**
• **Does this mean all kinds of dancing, or is one kind of dancing better than another?**

Fortunately, over decades, it has been shown that we increase our mental capacity by exercising our cognitive processes. Intelligence: Use it or lose it. Let us understand the bigger picture.

The essence of intelligence is making decisions. The best advice when it comes to improving your mental acuity is to involve yourself in activities which require split-second rapid-fire decision making, as opposed to rote memory (retracing the same well-worn paths), or just working on your physical style.

One way to do that is to learn something new. Not just dancing, but anything new. Don't worry about the probability that you'll never use it in the future. Take a class to challenge your mind. It will stimulate the connectivity of your brain by generating the need for new pathways. Difficult classes are better for you, as they will create a greater need for new neural pathways.

Then take a dance class, which can be even more effective. **Dancing integrates several brain functions at once — kinesthetic, rational, musical, and emotional — further increasing your neural connectivity.**

What kind of dancing?
Do *all* kinds of dancing lead to increased mental acuity? No, not all forms of dancing will produce the same benefit, especially if they only work on style, or merely retrace the same memorised paths. Making as many split-second decisions as possible, is the key to maintaining our cognitive abilities. Remember: intelligence is what we use when we don't already know what to do.

30 years ago the Albert Einstein College of Medicine thought of doing side-by-side comparisons of different kinds of dancing, to find out which was better. But we can figure it out by looking at who they studied: senior citizens of 75 and older, beginning in 1980. Those who danced in that particular population were former Roaring Twenties dancers (back in 1980) and then former Swing Era dancers (today), so the kind of dancing most of them continued to do in retirement was what they began when they were young: freestyle social dancing -- basic foxtrot, waltz, swing, and maybe some rumba and cha cha.

I've been watching senior citizens dance all of my life, from my parents (who met at a Tommy Dorsey dance), to retirement communities, to the Roseland Ballroom in New York. I almost never see memorised sequences or patterns on the dance floor. I mostly see easygoing, fairly simple social dancing — freestyle lead and follow. But freestyle social dancing isn't that simple! It requires a lot of split-second decision-making, in both the Lead and Follow roles.

Read more about the differences between the *three different kinds of ballroom dancing here*, to gain a better understanding of the role of decision-making in social or ballroom dance.

Social   Competitive   Exhibition

Which one is better?

Yes, that question is intentionally provocative, and is easily answered. All three forms are valid, each enjoyed by their adherents for good reasons. But it's helpful to know how and why they differ from each other. As you'll see in the third section below, it's sometimes essential to know the differences.

First, what is Ballroom Dance?

'Ballroom dance' refers to traditional partnered dance forms that are enjoyed by a couple, often in the embrace of closed dance position ('ballroom dance position'). These include waltz, swing, tango, salsa and blues.

'Ballroom dance' is the overall umbrella term, covering all three forms discussed on this page.

Social dance forms are important. The earliest historical dance forms ever described in writing were partnered social dances. Many of today's performative dance forms, including ballet and jazz dance, evolved from social dance forms that came first. And today, noncompetitive social dance continues to be the most widely practised form of dance in the world.

The three worlds of ballroom dance share the same historical roots, similar step vocabulary and music, so the three forms are considered siblings, related by birth. Yes, siblings are known to fight, but they can also be mutually supportive.

What is the essential difference between the three?

The main distinction is that they have **different audiences.**

Who are you dancing for, beyond your own enjoyment?

Social Ballroom	Competitive Ballroom	Exhibition Bathroom
Your Partner	The judges	An audience

Then looking closer at the differences.

What are your audience's expectations?

Your partners want to interact with you spontaneously, for fun, doing steps that are also enjoyable for them.	Judges want to see that the steps and styles are done precisely and correctly, with great flair.	Audiences want to be entertained, often with a preference for beautiful and impressive moves.

What is your focus?

It's how a dance feels to you and your partner, not how it looks. The experience.	It's how your dancing looks, for the judges. The appearance.	It's also how your dancing looks, for the audience. The appearance.

What is your attitude?

Sociable, which means friendly and kind.

Flexibly adaptive. You value and accommodate to styles that are different from your own.

Rigorously correct, expansive. · The many styles outside of the official syllabus are usually considered to be incorrect.

Performance attitude varies widely, depending on the dance form.

What is the attitude concerning mistakes?

Mistakes are accepted as inevitable. Social dancers laugh them off and move on.

When a Follow does something different from what the Lead intended, he knows it's a valid alternative interpretation of his lead.

Social dancers are happy if things work out 80% of the time. And the other 20% is when most learning happens.

Judges deduct points for every mistake, so competitive dance culture is aligned against making mistakes from day one. · When a Follow does something different from what the Lead intended, he considers it a mistake, which is to be eliminated. · Competitive dancers work hard to achieve 100%.

For professional performances, audiences expect perfection, so dance companies rehearse extensively to avoid any mistakes onstage. · For amateur performances, audiences mostly want to see that the dancers are enjoying themselves, so mistakes are generally accepted.

What is your reward?

The spontaneous enjoyment of improvising with a partner.

The satisfaction of becoming proficient in a dance form.

Self confidence.

Competing. Impressing others. Winning.

The satisfaction of becoming proficient in a dance form.

Self confidence.

Entertaining or impressing others. Enthusiastic applause.

The satisfaction of becoming proficient in a dance form.

Self confidence.

Are there standardised steps and technique?

No, standardisation doesn't function because each partner is different. You must modify your steps to adapt to each partner

Yes, rigorously standardised, because competitors need to know exactly what technical details the judges expect to see.

Sometimes, but in today's sampling culture ('been there, seen that') audiences prefer something they've never seen before.

Is there a standardised style?

Absolutely not. You develop your own *personal style*, different from others. Some social forms like swing, salsa and blues especially discourage copying others styles.

Yes, you are trained to copy the style of champions before you, working hard to imitate the shape of that standardised style. Individuality can be admired, but only within strict parameters.

Styles may be unique to the choreographer, thus not standardised. But the performing group usually works on copying and mastering that one style, in unison.

Is there a fixed choreography?

No. You make it up as you go, often based on what the Follow is doing at the moment, and what spontaneously occurs to the Lead. Both Lead and Follow engage in a highly active attention to possibilities.

Yes. Competitors usually perform choreographed routines that they have rehearsed.

An exception is Jack and Jill competitions,(partner dancing, where the competing couples are the result of random matching of leaders and follower) especially in WCS (West Coast Swing) and Lindy hop, with a partner where one has not danced with before.

Yes. Exhibitions are usually choreographed and rehearsed. Furthermore group routines often have everyone dancing in unison. But improvised exhibitions occasionally exist in swing, tango and blues.

Do you make your own decisions?

Yes, both Lead and Follow roles are continually engaged in split-second decision-making.	Usually not. Most decisions have been made by others, first in the syllabus of acceptable steps, then in the choreographed routine.	Not often. Most decisions have usually been made by the choreographers, and you work mostly on style.

Difficulty of technique

To state the obvious, competitive ballroom technique is designed for competitions. If dance technique is easy, judges won't be able to separate the good dancers from the very best. Therefore, competitive ballroom technique is intentionally difficult, so that only the very best dancers can master it. It requires many years, and extreme focus, to master this technique. U.S. Ballroom Dance Champion Stephen Hannah said, 'You must want to go to the very top and be the very best dancer. You must be able to use your time seven days a week without allowing any other influences to interfere.' This is not a problem. Competition ballroom dance is also known as DanceSport, and competitors in every sport train hard to win. It's work, and competitions are usually stressful.

Conversely, social ballroom technique is intentionally easy. Dance partnering is challenging enough as it is, to coordinate one's movements with another person. And most people want to dance with their friends as soon as possible. Therefore social dance technique is intentionally expedient, so that dancers can focus on the connection to their partners instead of intricate footwork technique and a highly specified style. It's play, and well known to be effective stress relief.

Repertoire of dances

The repertoire of International Style ballroom dance (the dominant competition form) was last revised around 1960. The ten

International Style ballroom dances are:

Slow Waltz • Viennese Waltz • Slow Foxtrot • Quickstep • Jive
Paso Doble • Tango • Samba • Cha-Cha • Rumba

Sixty years later, almost half of those have disappeared from social dancing.

Noncompetitive social dances are constantly updated. These include:

Lindy Hop • West Coast Swing • East Coast Swing • Hustle
Nightclub Two-Step • Cross-Step Waltz • Rotary Waltz
Country Waltz • Viennese Waltz • Polka • Salsa • Cha Cha
Bachata • Merengue • Kizomba • Social • Tango • Tango
Argentino • Blues Fusion

and many more.

The number of social dances increases each decade.

Other social dances

Not all social dances are social ballroom. Other social dance forms include hip-hop, breaking, line dances, international folk dance, contradancing, square dancing, grinding (yes, we need to include that), and informal permutations that defy categorization. This page focuses on the three worlds of ballroom dance, but acknowledges the many facets of social dance.

At this point, I want to clarify that I'm not demonising memorised sequence dancing, or style-focused pattern-based ballroom dancing. Although they don't have much influence on cognitive reserve, there are stress-reduction benefits from any kind of dancing, cardiovascular benefits to physical exercise, and even further benefits of feeling connected to a community of dancers. So, all dancing is good.

But when it comes to preserving (and improving) our mental acuity, then some forms are significantly better than others. While all dancing requires some intelligence, I encourage you to use your full intelligence when dancing, in both the Lead and Follow roles. The more decision-making we can bring into our dancing, the better.

Who benefits more, women or men?

In social dancing, the Follow role automatically gains a benefit, by making hundreds of split-second decisions as to what to do next, sometimes unconsciously, they don't 'follow', but interpret the signals their partners are giving them, and this requires intelligence and decision-making, which is active, not passive.

This benefit is greatly enhanced by dancing with different partners, not always with the same. With different dance partners, you have to adjust much more and be aware of more variables. This is great for staying smarter longer.

But you can also match the degree of decision-making if you choose to do so.

Here's how:

1) Really pay attention to your partner and what works best for them. Notice what is comfortable for them, where they are already going, which signals are successful and which aren't, and constantly adapt your dancing to these observations. That's rapid-fire split-second decision making.

2) Don't lead the same old patterns the same way each time. Challenge yourself to try new things each time you dance. Make more decisions more often. Intelligence: use it or lose it.

A huge side-benefit is that your partners will have much more fun dancing with you when you are attentive to their dancing and constantly adjusting for their comfort and continuity of motion. And as a result, you'll have more fun too.

Full engagement

Those who fully utilise their intelligence in dancing, at all levels, love the way it feels. Spontaneous leading and following both involve entering a flow state. Both leading and following benefit from a highly active attention to possibilities.

That's the most succinct definition I know for intelligent dancing: a highly active attention to possibilities. And I think it's wonderful that both the Lead and Follow role share this same ideal.

The best Leads appreciate the many options that the Follow must consider every second, and respect and appreciate the Follow's input into the collaboration of partner dancing. The Follow is finely attuned to the here-and-now in relaxed responsiveness, and so is the Lead.

Once this highly active attention to possibilities, flexibility, and alert tranquility are perfected in the art of dance partnering, dancers find it even more beneficial in their other relationships, and in everyday life.

Dance often

Another important suggestion: do it often. Seniors who did crossword puzzles four days a week had a measurably lower risk of dementia than those who did the puzzles once a week. If you can't take classes or go out dancing four times a week, then dance as much as you can. More is better.

And do it now, the sooner the better. It's essential to start building your cognitive reserve now. Someday you'll need as many of those stepping stones across the creek as possible. Don't wait — start building them now.

The past pages in this chapter are from writings by Richard Powers. He has such insight and has been teaching historic and contemporary social dance for many years. I really appreciate that he agreed for his observations to be included. For more from him, see https://www.richardpowers.com

So dance often!

Please read next about International Dance Day in an article in 2021 by Jenny Davies, author at *The Breaker*.

The Breaker is the news and features site run by the journalism master's students of the School of Journalism, English and Communication, Bournemouth University, England.

The world marks International Dance Day with dancers across the globe celebrating their passion for the art.

Whilst many forms of dancing are known to be great ways to stay physically healthy, the conversation this year has turned to how it can also help mental health too.

According to MindWise, in Belfast, Northern Ireland, dancing can both boost mood and contribute to the forming of new healthy habits. It has social benefits too, such as providing an opportunity to connect to others, which is positive for self esteem and improvement in mood.

Psychotherapist Terry Hyde, a trained ballet dancer and musical theatre performer who has worked with stars such as Barbara Streisand and Michael Crawford, explains how trying several new types of dance can be beneficial. He says:

'I've been suggesting to my therapy clients if you already do ballet, why not try something different? No one's going to see you. Try some tap, try some contemporary, try some musical theatre, try some singing lessons! All of these things are online free at the moment, try something different and that will take a bit of the anxiety away. It all boils down to identity…'

Although lockdowns have made it difficult for dancers to resume their usual activities, many dance companies are still offering online classes as well as online tutorials, where viewers can follow along at their own pace. Whilst it is suggested that anyone suffering from mental health worries still see a trained therapist, Hyde suggests that dancing can be an aid in your recovery. Sasha Bonewell, a graduate in dance at Buckinghamshire New University, in the UK, states that dance has been a great escape for her in times when she felt low. She says:

'Dancing is really enjoyable, and it can be good for your mental health. First of all, it's exercise so it releases a lot of endorphins, and it can make you feel really positive about yourself when you finally manage to get something right. The long days can be quite tiring, but you know how rewarding it is at the end and it really helps your self-esteem grow.'

Whether you celebrate International Dance Day or not, remember that any movement or exercise is great for your mental health and emotional wellbeing.

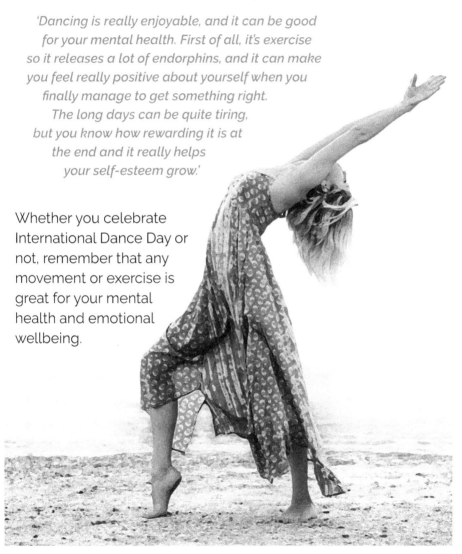

Chapter 7

Dance and multiple abilities

The amazing impact dance can have on people with special needs is very close to my heart. My mother's sister, my very dear Aunty Rae had cerebral palsy. A group of disorders that affects a person's ability to move and maintain balance and posture. Nevertheless, she had an amazing memory and fabulous sense of humour. She was born in 1920 and I know she attended ballet classes with my mother when they were little. Then, there was little understanding of disabilities and there weren't the same opportunities for her as she grew up, as there are for people today. Today dance is an inclusive sport and art, and there is no reason to leave anyone out on the grounds of disability. In 1997 I established *Charity Productions*, which was subsequently registered as *We Can Dance* to enable young people with special educational needs, such as profound and multiple learning difficulties, autism, physical disabilities, sensory impairments and behavioural difficulties, to access dance opportunities.

The charity aims to give children and young people with special educational needs the opportunity to access dance through professional teachers mainly trained by

Happy faces greeted HRH The Countess of Wessex when she visited a class at The Forest School in Knaresborough, Yorkshire, UK. The Charity We Can Dance funds dance lessons in 17 Special Needs Schools throughout the North of England. The Countess enjoyed watching a class of primary children led by one of the charity's 10 professional teachers. The smiles of the dancers (and the audience) said it all. After enjoying a wonderful dance class followed by a performance and proud bows. The Countess of Wessex was presented with a posy.

the *Royal Academy of Dance* and the *British Association of Teachers of Dancing*. The charity funds regular dance lessons within schools in North Yorkshire, County Durham and Teesside and also one- and two- day workshops during term-time. The instructors have experience in teaching children with special needs, and classes are planned to give students a great sense of achievement.

So, the benefits are many. From the joy of being able to express creativity and emotion, to the physical benefits of moving purposefully to the interpersonal rewards of working as a team to create something, to the cognitive benefits of working with music. Dance is a low-barrier way to enjoyment and stimulation for all of us, whatever our physical or mental capacities. Dance does not discriminate.

The performance of Andrew Self, a 21-year-old star of UK TV show *The Greatest Dancer*, illustrates just how dance can transform lives. Andrew has Down's syndrome, and his mother explains:

'Andrew is quite flat-footed when he walks, but the change in him when he dances is quite amazing. He's literally born to dance - it's just transformed his life and I would add that dance has given him so much confidence - when I look at his first performances the difference is remarkable.'

Andrew himself explains how dance shows him that Down's syndrome doesn't stop him doing ANYTHING.

In an RAD Twitter post this comment (unattributed) is evocative:

'As a young kid with audio dyslexia, crippling shyness, bad scoliosis and low self-esteem, dance was not just a nice activity, it was life changing. It helped me find my voice, get control of my body and develop mental resilience. Get kids dancing as much as possible!'

Dance and degenerative conditions

Parkinson's disease is a progressive neurodegenerative condition that affects movement – usually the first signs are shaking, stiffness and difficulty moving. Because music acts as a movement cue in dancing, it triggers the brain to use a different pathway, meaning many people with Parkinson's don't experience shaking in the same way when they move to music. Outside of dance classes, participants tend to experience fewer symptoms as well. The 'Dance For Parkinson's' programme, which is available in different countries, combines tailored physical exercise, mental stimulation and social stimulation to support people with the disease. One of the founders of the American programme, David Leventhal, of Brooklyn, NY says:

'The fundamentals of dancing and dance training—things like balance, movement sequencing, rhythm, spatial and aesthetic awareness, and dynamic coordination—seem to address many of the things people with Parkinson's want to work on to maintain a sense of confidence and grace in their movements. Although participants from all over the world tell us they find elements of the class therapeutic, the primary goal of our program is for people to enjoy dance for dancing's sake in a group setting—and to explore the range of physical, artistic and creative possibilities that are still very much open to them.'

The Sarasota Ballet, in Florida, USA, champions the view that dance is for all. While working there, I observed many of their programmes

which are extremely well attended. Everyone has a positive experience. One of the programs they run is *Joyful Movement Through Parkinson's*. The company says:

> *'The Sarasota Ballet is proud to offer Joyful Movement Through Parkinson's in partnership with the Neuro Challenge Foundation for Parkinson's. In this interactive class, students enjoy an exploration into the beautiful world of ballet through movement, creativity, and music. Each class begins with a gentle warm-up and stretching of the body, followed by balletic movements that relate to actual ballets being performed by The Sarasota Ballet Company. Students will also discover the history of each ballet. Joyful Movement Through Parkinson's is a wonderful chance to exercise in a unique way: classes help with range of motion, coordination, and mobility.'*

It's education director, Christopher Hird, one of the leaders on the course, says:

> *'We are privileged to be part of this amazing program here in Sarasota and share our love of dance and particularly ballet with our local Parkinson's community.'*

I want to share the story of Elizabeth Twistington Higgins MBE (1923 – 1990). She was a British ballet dancer, and later a painter. I thought here would be a great place to add this story. I have read the wonderful book about her life and art by Mark Alexander and I can thoroughly recommend it. It shows how dance can influence someone to make the most of life despite adversity, hardships and extreme difficulty. She was fêted in an episode of *This is Your Life*, a UK television show presented by Eamonn Andrews who surprised her at the Middlesex Hospital in London. The book *The Dance goes on: The life and art of Elizabeth Twistington Higgins*, has a forward by HRH the late Prince Philip, Duke of Edinburgh. He was full of admiration for this amazing lady. She found dance carried her through the most difficult time of her life.

Elizabeth trained with the Sadler's Wells Ballet School, and took dancing lessons with the Arts Educational Trust, or Arts Ed, where she later worked as a teacher. At the height of her career as a classical ballet dancer she was struck down by paralytic polio in 1953. Totally immobilised, Elizabeth was confined to a wheelchair by day and slept in an iron lung by night. Despite being almost totally paralysed from the neck down, she established her own dance group and became a successful painter by mouth.

Elizabeth recalls her experience of *This Is Your Life*:

'My birthday in 1961 is firmly etched in my memory. I was asked by the BBC to appear in **Town and Around**, a daily magazine programme about the South East of England. When they suggested that I went to London for the interview, I was a bit suspicious. In normal circumstances, a mobile camera team would have come to Dover. My suspicions were well-founded; this was only a ruse to get me to appear on the weekly programme. **This Is Your Life**, which gave a glimpse into the lives of celebrated or interesting people. I was amazed that they should consider me a suitable subject.

An appearance on **This Is Your Life** was supposed to come as a complete surprise, but my doctor had advised the producer not to spring a sudden shock on me. I was shocked. I burst into tears. I felt I could not face my friends and relations saying kind and flattering things about me for half an hour. Overwhelming kindness always upset me.

I told Matron I could not do it. She seemed very disappointed, but I think she understood. I was glad she was the only person who witnessed my emotional outburst. She left, saying that the decision was entirely up to me; I was to think it over and let her know in the morning.

This bombshell interrupted a painting lesson with Rosemary, my friend, and had completely shattered my powers of concentration.

There was no more work that afternoon.

I discovered that Rosemary, was already in on the secret, and she spent the rest of the afternoon calming me down. She told me that, of the four lives prepared for the following week, three had left the country. If I did not appear, the programme would either have to be cancelled or a repeat performance shown. She was very persuasive. I felt I could not let everyone down and accepted the challenge, though reluctantly. I had accepted challenges before, but this one scared me stiff. In the theatre, I would have given my bottom dollar for this kind of publicity. Now I was in a wheelchair. I did not want to appear before an audience.

The nurses knew that something was troubling me but, as I was under a vow of silence, it was impossible for me to communicate with them. I could not eat or sleep or concentrate; my thoughts were focused entirely on the ordeal ahead. My mind was so preoccupied that I never even thought of buying anything special to wear on this great occasion. Looking back, I am still amazed at myself – it was so unlike me. I felt sick with anxiety and nerves and the next four days seemed endless.

On the fifth of November, I was formally admitted to the Observation Ward of the Middlesex Hospital in London. Here too, secrecy prevailed, and I was obviously a rather mysterious patient. I was under the care of the Regional Medical Officer, and his young Houseman thought I was an interesting case. After asking me a lot of questions about my illness, he looked incredulously at me and said, 'You're a living miracle!' This was his first meeting with someone who had had respiratory polio.

Early the next morning, the BBC took possession of my room. Everything was moved out of the way; cameras brought in, cables laid, lights fixed, sound tested; the interviewer, Nancy Wise, came in and we were on the air.

The conversation that followed was spontaneous and went off quite well, apart from one rather awkward moment.

'Do you miss the world of ballet?'

For a second, I was completely taken aback by such an obvious query, and sharply retorted,

'Of course, I do!'

This was not very polite of me and Nancy must have felt terrible having asked such a tactless question. I have always been a volatile and emotional person. If only I could react more slowly and had greater control over my emotions, I would so often save others from being hurt and embarrassed.

At the end of the interview, Nancy said to me, 'As it is your birthday Elizabeth, the BBC has prepared a surprise for you.'

She turned to face the door and in walked Eamonn Andrews.

After a few words of greeting, he asked me if I would come to the Television Theatre that evening and see what other surprises the BBC had in store for me.

I spent the afternoon resting in my respirator. I was being washed and dressed for the evening performance when our pre-recorded interview was shown in 'Town and Around'. I did not see myself, nor did I hear Eamonn Andrews say that, for the first time they were breaking the usual rule of silence for the evening's performance of This Is Your Life. Owing to my disabilities, it had been decided to warn me beforehand that I would be appearing. There must be a story behind the life of every disabled person. That mine was chosen to be shown on television was for its visual appeal, and because it was easy for people to realise the enormous change from dancing on stage to a life of immobility in a wheelchair. There was no doubt at all that the public's imagination had been captured. Not *only those leading a normal life, but disabled people too, known and unknown, wrote to me. The programme, they said, had been inspiring and encouraged them to new efforts. I was surprised and felt very humble. It had never occurred to me that my struggles to paint could have helped others in this way. It was one of the unexpected rewards. The other came a few weeks later. A special despatch rider drove up to the hospital with an enormous red morocco-bound book of photographs – a wonderful souvenir of an unusual and very happy birthday.'*

In her book you can read the whole story. Elizabeth went on to run her own ballet company, the Chelmsford Ballet Company, in Chelmsford,UK, and choreographed for it.

Thank you for this tribute and these very special words written by one of Elizabeth Twistington Higgin's pupil, Pip Marsh.

I understand that Pip found writing surprisingly emotional. She went on to a very successful professional career with The Royal Ballet. The story would make any teacher proud. Pip writes:

'I was taught by 'Miss Elizabeth', as I called her, between the ages of 10 and 11. I would have a private lesson with her once a week in her beautiful studio that opened onto her garden.

By this point she was living with an iron lung in her home so that she no longer had to travel to hospital every night. She had 24 hour care and her wheelchair gifted her her independence. It allowed her to answer the phone, answer the door, call for her assistant, and work the tape machine she used for our classes.

She was a formidable woman, not just in the eyes of a 10 year old and a true inspiration. She was a brilliant teacher despite her paralysis. With the help of one of her dancers, Sheila Large, I learnt more in that year than I could ever thank her for. With her knowledge and guidance I obtained a place at The Royal Ballet School, became a member of The Royal Ballet in 1991 and 8 years later joined Matthew Bourne's Adventures in Motion Pictures (now New Adventures). She gave me one of her paintings as a good luck gift for joining the Royal Ballet School. It depicts three dancers posing as Mary and two angels and she wrote to me that she hoped that these guardian angels would watch over me.

Pip Marsh, as a child, standing next to Elizabeth Twistington Higgins. Sheila Large in the background.

I truly believe that I would not have had the career I did without her. Because she only had her words to describe what she wanted from me, it switched on a part of my brain that proved invaluable as a dancer. I was able to learn choreography very quickly and became a reliable member of the company who could be thrown on at a moment's notice.

A painting given to Pip by Elizabeth Twistington Higgins

Miss Elizabeth passed away when I was 17 while I was still training at The Royal Ballet School so sadly she didn't get to know of my success. I will forever be grateful for her belief in me and being an incredible role model for a young girl following her dream. She taught me to be determined, hard-working, and just like her, to never give up no matter what life throws at you.'

Indeed there is so much more to dance than mastering steps. And it has its role to play in the classroom too, as we will see next.

Chapter 8

Get dancing!

Over the previous chapters we have seen how dance can be woven into every facet of our life. From the role it has played in societies around the world since early civilisation, to the importance for our education, skills development and wellbeing, the benefits of dance are all around us.

Hopefully the stories and the research shared here have inspired you to bring more dancing into your life. But

how? This chapter shares some very simple steps for getting started: the how, what, where and when as well as a gentle reminder of 'why'. Everything you need to get your dancing started!

How to get started

If dancing has not been a part of your world, ever, or dormant for some time, perhaps the biggest question you will have is how to bring it into your life. Perhaps there are unspoken fears still to overcome.

Overcoming mental barriers

Think back to the exercise at the start of the book, when you were asked to note all the stories, experiences, and associations you have with dance. Hopefully you will have some happy memories, but for some there will also still be a sense of fear, embarrassment or it's not for me or, not for my children, when it comes to moving our bodies rhythmically. Some of these fears, are based in myths and untruths.

I'm too old, unfit, uncoordinated?

If you associate dance with performance on stage, you may think you don't have what it takes to get dancing. If so, you are viewing dance through a very narrow lens. The Oxford Dictionary's definition of dance is simply 'moving rhythmically to music'. The beauty of dance is that it's available to all of us! No-one expects a beginner to quickly master the steps, whatever their age. The heart of dance lies in the joy of the experience – the having fun, not what you look like. Aubrey Lynch, life coach, chief education & creative programs officer at the Harlem School of Arts, New York, presenter of Life Lessons, and a choreographer says:

"To touch, to move, to inspire. That is the true gift of dance."

Here is his narrative.

The Aubrey Lynch story...

Straight out of Michigan, with a very late start at age 16, he set foot into New York City to start a dance career, where he became one of the last dancers chosen by Alvin Ailey, a choreographer who founded the Alvin Ailey American Dance Theater in 1958. After several seasons with the Ailey Company, Aubrey ventured into the commercial world, becoming an original cast member of the iconic Broadway musical, The Lion King, and rising through the ranks from dance captain, associate choreographer, to associate producer. He developed a curriculum 'The Aubrey

Lynch Experience' which aims to teach important life lessons to students of the arts. For the class nerd who was one of the few black students in his senior school, where he was bullied, his accomplishments through dance have been amazing.

A quote he trademarked is: 'The arts aren't extracurricular; they are extra essential.' It means the arts isn't something we do in our spare time, if we have time. The arts is like air, bread, and water. You have to have the arts at some level of your life. Many problems we have in the world are just unfocused art.'

So, the first person you move and inspire is yourself.

People will laugh

This fear that you will make a fool of yourself can be a nagging worry. Perhaps you have experienced teasing in the school playground, or power plays in the workplace. The wonderful thing about dance is that it avoids these scenarios. In a dance class, everyone is there for the same reason. People are there to support each other, not bring each other down, as we have seen in some of the inspiring stories shared by our contributors earlier in this book. With children, an attentive dance teacher will cultivate a culture of respect and support in their classes. Even in informal dance settings

such as at a wedding or in a club, if there is laughter, it stems from a communal bond, from everyone having fun, rather than harsh judgement. There's a saying that 'people who dance together, stay together' that has a lot of truth in it!

Dance is not for boys and men

Hopefully this is a myth that has been firmly quashed in the 21st century. Nevertheless, I still hear of parents who are reluctant to enrol their boys into dance classes, or men who would secretly love to dance but feel self-conscious.

Dance is for everyone. Many dance styles (such as ballroom, street dance and Latin American) require roles for men, and dance classes are full of women pairing up because of a dearth of males. As for younger boys, what a shame to rob them of the life skills that dance can bring simply because of outdated stereotypes. More boys are entering the dance world all the time and reaping the benefits.

Jasmine Wilson, trained as a dancer, is Director of Learning and Engagement for Wayne McGregor CBE.* She delivers and manages workshops and strategy, alongside the main company work and how

* Wayne McGregor is a multi-award-winning British choreographer and director, internationally renowned for trailblazing innovations in performance that have radically redefined dance in the modern era.

it sits in the wider arts and educational context. Jasmine says:

'...as part of a patchwork - The Place, which is the UK's premiere centre for contemporary dance uniting dance training, creation and performance in its unique, purpose-built centre, and The Dance Umbrella, which is London's international dance festival, celebrating 21st century choreography across the capital and beyond, and us - we work in partnership to signpost and work with young people. It's for young persons moving into the profession and also working on community based projects, trying to build links with community in East London at real grass root level. One of the things that struck me when we sent out flyers to locals across East London, an elderly man turned up for exercise class, he didn't come for dance but now he's attended every session and even though he seems very ill, his doctor encouraged him to relieve stress and suggested exercise. Now he's creating choreography and doing work. He's realised he has a flexible body and can nearly do the splits. He hasn't done sport or anything in the past and now he can connect fully with his body even though it is failing him in other ways. It has become a special part of his life.'

If this man had been introduced to dance earlier, his life would have been so different.

Overcoming practical barriers

If you have no fear about dancing, you may still struggle to take the first step if you don't know where to start. We will tackle some of these stumbling blocks in the rest of the chapter, but rest assured, there is a way to bring more dancing into your life, whatever your lifestyle restrictions!

Friday 13th is always a special day for me. Great things happen. It was one such day that I discovered this article by Jan Masters. She responded to my email saying she was happy to be quoted and kindly sent this fabulous photo of her in a dance studio.

She exemplifies and puts succinctly everything you have been reading about so far and why it's time to put on your dancing shoes. Read on.

The Telegraph Magazine columnist Jan Masters explains in one of her weekly series: *What is 60 for?*

There's nothing like dance for keeping you on your toes in every way.

What is 60 for?

Article from Telegraph Magazine 14 May 2022 by Jan Masters

One by one, we find a place at the barre. Usually the same place. We are creatures of habit. We wriggle our feet into ballet shoes (not tippy-toe pointe shoes but canvas or leather flats). Some students embark on serious stretching. I touch my toes, then chat. Welcome to my grown-up ballet class, one of my favourite ways to exercise and unwind.

'General level' is how the lesson is billed, which means that it's for mixed abilities. But ability is not the only thing that varies. We're all different shapes, sizes and ages. Granted, I'm at the older end of the scale, but no one gives age a second thought (it's not as though we're striving for stardom at the Royal Opera House). And oh, how I love the absolute freedom to move across the expanse of a studio floor. To interpret music through movement; to dance in space and in sync with others. These are the moments when my rampant anxiety seems to disappear, exiting stage left.

I've dipped in and out of ballet all my life, and lessons still run to much the same format as they did when I was six years old and attending classes over the Co-op, run by the formidable Mrs Gray, accompanied by Mrs Bungard on the ivories. Each year, an examiner would descend from the Royal Academy of Dance to sit at a spindly table, pen poised, inviting entrants into the examination room by ringing a small hand bell. God, that bell. For us quivering fairies it had all the ominous gravitas of the gong at the start of a Rank feature film.

I did terribly well at RAD exams but I chucked in the towel in my early teens, when Mrs Gray decamped to the church hall, which meant that boys from the fifth form could peer in through the windows and take the mickey. It was silly of me to pack it in. Message to the young: don't base any life choices on the sniggerings of schoolboys.

Now, I find ballet classes akin to meditation. First, because the music, whether pre-recorded or played live by a pianist, is so spirit-lifting – it might be Tchaikovsky, it might be a classical take on The Flintstones, but it's a fast ticket out of reality.

Secondly, the very nature of the exercises means that you have to put your worries to one side and concentrate hard. Because while the individual steps correspond to a learnt universal language, the order in which the teacher links them together changes every time. All you get is a quick demo, an even faster recap – and you're on. It's daunting, but it's superb training for your memory.

In fact, it has been found that dancing – for example, ballroom, Latin or salsa – can raise mood, increase flexibility and support cognition in healthy older adults. The multisensory stimulation and social interaction, coupled with learning new sequences of movements, perhaps while anticipating and reacting to cues from a partner, can bolster brain health.

One landmark study looked at people over 40 without cardiovascular disease and found those who participated in regular dancing over the following decade almost halved their risk of dying from the disease. For this benefit, you gotta get a bit sweaty and out of breath, though – sitting on the floor for Oops Upside Your Head won't cut it.

Having travelled a lot, I've come to realise that dance is something humans everywhere are compelled to do. It's as if it's in our DNA. Which is why wherever I may be on a trip, to truly put a finger on the pulse of a place, I seek out the local dance scene.

No, I'm not talking hotel foyer shows where every night a trio duly don nylon costumes and execute some bendy tricks with a ewer balanced on the forehead, before encouraging audience participation (why is it trapped tourists always seem to do the same gyrations, wafting limp arms in no particular rhythmic relationship to their hapless jigging about?). What I'm referring to is feeling the heartbeat of a neighbourhood. For example, in Buenos Aires, my husband and I skip the slick tango shows and instead seek out the milongas, tango events that seldom get going before midnight, at which all ages partner each other.

I wish that, as a nation, we danced more. Together. Sure, if you're young, there are clubs and raves (in my day, the equivalent was the D-I-S-C-O, where we freestyled to I Feel Love by Donna Summer), and yes, dance is growing in popularity. But for many mature types, the nearest they get is watching Strictly or bopping to Dancing Queen at a wedding reception.

I believe more community dancing might contribute to our gross national happiness. I only have to see how much my friend and her husband, who must be in their 70s, enjoy Scottish dancing, reeling the night away. They show such stamina, such style, they're my poster children for the benefits of dance at any age.

What dancing is out there?

I was once a dance teacher at a mainstream school – a place that didn't really focus on dance. The students there knew very little about dancing and held the view that it was something other people did, usually on stage and in tutus. I had to show them that there was more to dance than meets the eye and used the image of an umbrella to show the diversity of dancing styles, with each panel of the umbrella representing a different type of dance. This was the very first dance umbrella that I created!

When I researched this more deeply, I found over 500 dance styles – that would have been a difficult umbrella to draw on a classroom board! But it goes to show how there is a style of dance for everyone. Finding one to suit you is simply a matter of exploration and experimentation. As a very rough guide, these are some of the styles that might work for you.

If you are mainly looking for: -

Structure and progress

If you would like to learn a dance technique from the start and make progress over time, ballet, jazz, modern or tap classes may suit you. You will start with learning the foundations of the dance style and slowly start to build on these over time. You will find links to associations at the end of this chapter.

A sociable time

Line dancing presents itself as an ideal form of exercise for older people because it provides the benefits of an aerobic workout, helping to maintain a healthy heart and also provides a platform for you to get involved in a social environment, which is great  for mental wellness. Line Dancing is widely known to be one of the best forms of exercise for ageing bodies, as studies have shown. One such study was conducted by a professor of dance named Mynette Aguilar, Faculty Member of the University of the Philippines Diliman, College of Human Kinetics. The research shows that line dance helps improve cardiovascular health. It shows an overall lowering of the resting heart rate, which is known to be a large indicator of the general health of the heart.

Circle or Partner. Partner dances require a focus on technique, and you will be dancing with someone else. Often at the end of the class, or at certain times in the year, there are social dances where you can have a go with different partners and put your own steps together, rather than repeat routines. Circle dances tend to have less of a focus on technique and more on community and steps being passed down from generation to generation, so there is less emphasis on your footwork!

Belly dancing and tribal dancing for women can also be a very effective way of making new friends, as much of the meaning behind the dance is around female empowerment and community.

Scottish Country Dancing is said to help to prevent degenerative diseases like Alzheimer's. The need to be coordinated and keep up with timings keeps your brain engaged. It builds bone density, core strength and agility. It reduces stress and improves your mood. It is sometimes danced as solo, sometimes with a partner and sometimes in group formation.

Self-expression

Freestyle, modern stage and 5 rhythms are dance styles that enable you to bring your own creativity and expression to the fore. You will learn steps and techniques but often have the chance to put these together in your own style to the music.

Fitness

I would recommend all styles of dancing to improve fitness! Dance incorporates balance, strength and aerobic exercise in all forms, with the level adapted to suit the class. It is evident that dancing outranks standard exercise classes when it comes to positive outcomes for mental health too. Ostensibly due to the variety of movements on offer, and music being involved.

Don't limit yourself to the styles of dance mentioned here. There isn't space to feature all 500+ genres! The best thing to do is see what's available locally, by seeking recommendations from friends, looking online, in a local directory or asking in a library for sources of information. Then try out a class.

Many dance schools will allow you to take a trial class before committing yourself, so try out what's available until you find something that suits you! Generally, you will be able to access or try a complimentary 'first' class. Wear comfortable, breathable clothing too. Do not spend money on shoes or dance attire before you are ready. If budget is a problem, many dance schools have second-hand sales, or you can look online.

When: create the opportunity to dance

For some of us, the will to dance is there but it's a matter of fitting it in. Time is a problem for many of us, whether it's children with heavily committed social calendars or adults with too many caring or other responsibilities. Depending on where you live, fitting a class into your existing timetable may be difficult, so here are some tips about making space for dance in your life, whatever your circumstances:

Prioritise what's important

If you have decided that dance will be a valuable addition to your life, or a child's life, perhaps something else must make way for it. Think about whether there are existing activities that you could pause for a while to try dance instead. Perhaps your child has been going to an after-school class for years but would like to try something new. Or perhaps you can identify that you have time in the evenings that is usually spent watching TV, and you could fill that time slot with a dance class instead. You won't regret it. Read where I have suggested some simple exercises that could get you started from the comfort of your home.

It won't always be possible for you to create more time, but for many of us, a new interest or hobby is just the prompt we need to do a quick time audit and see where our precious hours are going! Where can you save time and let dance in?

Do it at home

Often when people think about dance, they assume it takes place in a class or dance studio setting. That doesn't need to be the case. Many of the health and wellbeing benefits of dance we have seen, apply as much to informal dancing as they do to partaking in class. If you can't spare an hour a week to commit to a class, try setting aside some time at home. Perhaps it might be five minutes a day to play your favourite music and simply enjoy dancing. Perhaps you could create an hour's slot once a week for your own dancing –

inviting friends to come along if you feel like it. There are plenty of online tutorials available now, via YouTube and other sources. I won't recommend any in particular as the online world moves so fast, but it is worth a look if you'd like to learn particular steps or styles from the comfort of your own kitchen!

Take opportunities

The only difference between a dancer and a non-dancer is whether they dance! You don't need a special induction or password to enter the dance world! So next time you are at a wedding, party, or other occasion where music is playing, get up and dance. Say yes to yourself, be brave enough to overcome the fears we talked about earlier.
You will become a positive role model to those about you too, who will be more inclined to dance once you do. Dancing is contagious! So, Dance for your life!

Why?

I want to dwell on the most important of questions – why dance? In a way, the whole book has tackled this question. We have unlocked the hidden transferable lifestyle skills learned through dance participation and looked at why dance has been so important across cultures through the ages, we have looked at the ways in which it develops life skills and enriches education and learning potential. And we have seen how vitally important it is for health – for degenerative conditions, for maintaining health as we age, for our emotional and mental wellbeing.

But I want to underline the point that the real magic of dance however lies in your own relationship with it, not in your ability or in finding a great teacher. Dance can be whatever you need it to be – an anchor point in your week when life is difficult, a route to fitness and happiness, a way of being yourself when you feel out of place in traditional schooling, and an opportunity to build lasting friendships.

That is why it is so important to come to dance with an open mind, and persevere until you find a class, genre or approach that suits you. As I have said before, unlike many sports, dance is not necessarily competitive.

The African-American choreographer, dancer and director Alvin Ailey 1931 – 1989 said:

'Dance is for everybody. I believe that the dance came from the people and that it should always be delivered back to the people.'

Where do we go from here?

Remembering that so many transferable life skills are absorbed by the dancer.

We have read so many stories of other people's journeys and ideas but, what about yours? Perhaps the next step is for you or someone you know. Or perhaps, you are a parent or caregiver interested in finding out more and which dance style will suit your child.

I have sought to list all the organisations that could help you. However, the list is not exhaustive.

So, let's get dancing now.

First, here are five movements that you can practise to get started. I have always been an advocate of taking things step by step, not trying to cram your brain with too much too soon.

SO...

All these basic steps can be done in the kitchen or sitting room or wherever you feel comfortable. Hold on gently to something about waist height. Start with feet parallel and standing straight, shoulders over hips, we always use both sides of the body, so first, right arm or foot then repeat with left. Notice that I say 8 repetitions, that's because music is generally counted in 4's and 8's. You can play some music... but that's not necessary. Try singing Happy Birthday twice for the first exercise!

demi pointe

1. Lift your heels *only* and rise-up onto your toes (Ballet term is **demi pointe**). Do this 8 times. About the time for the kettle to boil! Make sure you keep the balls of your feet in touch with the floor.

2. Bend knees and stretch 8 times (Ballet term is **demi plié**) keep heels touching the floor.

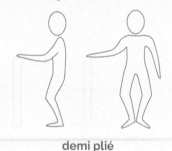

demi plié

3. Bring foot to knee and replace (Ballet term is **retiré**). 8 times with right 8 left.

retiré

4. Keeping shoulders relaxed, slowly lift arms up to the front of you -shoulder width apart- and take them to the side but not behind your body then lower to your side (Ballet term is **ports de bras**). Reach out with your fingers. Repeat 4 times.

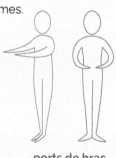

ports de bras

5. Slide your foot out to front till your foot is stretched to a point and return (Ballet term is **battement tendu**). Repeat 8 times with the right, 8 times with the left.

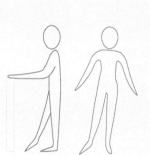

battement tendu

First

Next time try the same movements but start with your feet in a turned-out position (First position in Ballet). Imagine you are making the shape where a quarter of a piece of pizza could fit. Take care to keep knees over toes!

You can always mix and match these movements even transferring weight from one foot to another from the fifth movement.

I am also a STRONG advocate of engaging with a teacher, they are trained to help you and make sure you are exercising safely and correctly. Overcoming obstacles to exercising is normal. If you're having trouble beginning an exercise plan or following through, you're not alone. Many of us struggle getting out of our comfort zone. I will list here places to find something to suit you. If not please email me and I will point you in the right direction!

If you want to find a teacher, studio or just encouragement, do email me: suehewgillpeterson101@gmail.com I will always reply.

Or visit my website: www.suehewgillpeterson.com

To inspire you I have included a blog by Steve Sirico on *Dance Teacher Web*. I just had to include it. It was written in 2021.

A Tribute to Dance Teachers and Studio Owners Everywhere!

Think about this...

Dance teachers lift students up by giving them hope and inspiration through dance education!

No matter where you live in the world, I would be willing to bet you will find a dance studio in some town nearby. And while in many cases they may be taken for granted and some people in the town may not know anything about what goes on in these sacred establishments, we do!

Thousands of hours are spent on pliés, pas de bourrées, pirouettes, grand jetés, développés and that's only scratching the surface. There are many other styles of dance being taught in each dance studio by eager and passionate dance teachers who are sharing their love of dance. Students of all ages are developing strength, enhancing coordination, musicality, improving flexibility, balance and learning full dance routines and then having the courage to get on stage and perform!

But as dance teachers, we know that is only what people see on the outside. What dance training builds on the inside outweighs any step or dance routine learned. And that is for students of all ages! Important life enhancing skills are being propped up, reinforced and built. Improved self-esteem, problem solving skills and enhanced self-awareness. Having a better understanding of teamwork and realising that hard work can not only be fun but equals results. The synergy of all of this coming together is powerful to say the least. And these are just some of the all-important life lessons learned. After 30+ years of being a dance studio owner and dance teacher I have seen first-hand from alumni who come back to visit. From doctors to CEOs to lawyers, professional dancers, body builders and moms, they all attribute a big part of their growth, success and happiness in life to their time at our studio.

Yes, it is true. Dance studios are an important part of the fabric of any community.

They are an institution of higher education where children are not only learning the art of dance but the art of life. Dance education lifts students up, giving them hope and inspiration. Students who partake in dance lessons are better listeners. They also understand that everyone will have a unique way of self-expression and are more tolerant of people's differences. Yes, the education part is huge for these students and will leave an everlasting mark on their lives, but it doesn't end there!

Dance evokes inspiration and is something that gives joy and happiness as well as a spirit of hopefulness. It also creates awe in both the performer and the person watching. Studies have shown that experiencing awe and inspiration makes us more prone to positive behavour towards others. We are less likely to care exclusively about ourselves after experiencing the feeling of awe and we feel better connected as a part of a larger whole. It is a self-transcendent emotion alongside compassion and gratitude that some researchers believe helped us evolve as humans and gives us the ability to care for one another, cooperate and coordinate as a group.

Now, how important is that nowadays!

Studies by several universities have shown that students who are involved in the arts are:
3 times more likely to win an achievement award
4 times more likely to be recognised for outstanding leadership
5 times more likely to be promoted in the work force, demonstrate improved time management and lower dropout rates

And some people think we are just teaching dance steps!

The next time someone comes into your studio to question whether the time and money spent at the studio is worth it, feel free to share this article with them!

In light of what has transpired during the Covid-19 pandemic, dance teachers stepped up and helped on so many levels. Making sure their students continued to train remotely and enjoy some normalcy during that extraordinary time. Most studio owners and dance teachers were operating at a loss... A BIG LOSS! But they continued because they know and understand the importance of dance and the joy and love it brings to their students. And yes, we selfishly are also winning because teaching nourishes our souls and makes us feel whole again. But we also know that our students come first. Dance teachers are the most giving people I know. And not just of their expertise but of their love for their students.

Mentors, trainers, coaches and surrogate parents are just some of the labels I would use to describe a dance teacher. This truly is an honorable profession you are a part of and we salute you for all you have done and will be doing moving forward. People in your town should know all of this about you. It's time to spread the good word about your dance studio!

Nothing will compare to the life-long connection I have built with many amazing students who are now adults. I wouldn't trade in being a dance teacher and studio owner for anything.

I applaud you for all of your hard work so please take a bow and remember you do make a BIG difference in this world

Here's to your success!

All these words are by Steve Siroco. I applaud him for writing this blog.

Don't underestimate yourself. You are more than you think.

MISTY COPELAND

Here are some suggestions of how to proceed

You can also ask at your local **Library** or **Google** online.

International organisations for you to try:

Royal Academy of Dance (RAD) International organisation based in London. With over 15,500 members spread across 82 countries, the **RAD** is one of the largest and most influential dance education and training organisations in the world.

Classes and exams for ALL ages and genders.

Silver Swans classes for over 55s prove extremely popular throughout the world.

Boys and men's classes have special focus too.

Of course, the RAD is world renowned for children's classes and examinations. Well-known also for developing dancers for Ballet and Contemporary Companies across all continents. It's centenary was in 2020.

Website: https://www.royalacademyofdance.org/

Phone: +44 (0)20 7326 8000

Imperial Society of Teachers of Dancing (ISTD) Dance teachers of all styles. Including Ballroom Dance National Dance associations. With more than 7,000 members in over 65 countries around the world, ISTD offers a broad range of categories and benefits to members. From Ballet to Ballroom

Many dance faculties covering Theatre, Dancesport and Social Dance.

Cecchetti Classical Ballet	Disco, Freestyle & Rock 'n' Roll
Imperial Classical Ballet	Classical Greek
Classical Indian Dance	Modern Ballroom
Latin American	Modern Theatre
Contemporary Dance	National

Jazz

Sequence

Tap Dance

Street Dance

Website: https://www.istd.org/home

Phone: +44 (0)20 7377 1577

The American Ballet Theatre (ABT) With over 200 Affiliate Members with a National Ballet Curriculum. **ABT** is enhancing the training of American ballet dancers and teachers.

Website: https://www.abt.org/

British Ballet Organisation (BBO) Established in 1930, the **BBO** is justly proud of many members worldwide including Australia and New Zealand.

It offers a wide range of examinations and assessments for students of all ages and abilities, in the UK and internationally. Regulated by the Office of Qualifications and Examinations Regulation (Ofqual) and Qualifications Wales, **bbodance** exams are designed to support students to acquire good dance technique, artistry, and performance skills across a wide range of genres.

It's syllabus and examinations offer a broad education in and through dance that is accessible to all children, young people, and adults, with or without prior dance experience

bbodance holds many events each year across the globe. It's Continual Professional Development activities are designed to develop and nurture teaching skills. Student masterclasses of varying types give young dancers the opportunity to take part in exciting day courses taught by professionals in the dance world. Dance Days operates in the UK, Australia and New Zealand and gives members the chance to get together and experience an intensive course with industry professionals.

Website: https://bbo.dance/

Phone: 020 8748 1241

British Association of Teachers of Dancing (BATD)

The British Association is represented in the United Kingdom, Malta, Canada, America, Australia, South Africa, Spain, France, Italy, Holland, Germany, Belarus, Latvia, Korea and many other countries. It was founded in 1892.

Acro/Gymnastics	Highland Dance
Ballet	Jazz
Ballroom	Majorette
Cheer Pom	Modern Dance
Country and Western	Special Needs
European National	Step Dancing
Freestyle	Tap Dancing

Website: https://batd.co.uk/
Phone: 0141 427 3699

British Theatre Dance Association (BTDA) was founded in 1972 and has since expanded throughout the United Kingdom and several countries abroad.

BTDA is committed to ensuring access to all who have the capacity to safely participate in dance and offers a range of examinations and awards to recognise an individual's achievements.

Classical Ballet	Performance Awards
Modern Jazz	Bollywood
Tap Dance	Choreography
Acrobatic	Educational Freestyle
Lyrical	Modelling
Greek	National
Musical Theatre	Speech & Drama

Website: https://www.btda.org.uk/

The UK's Best Dance Schools – A Guide

Each year thousands of children from across the world audition for full-time ballet schools and colleges. We are fortunate in the UK to have some of the best training available in the world, producing top-class dancers.

Applying for and choosing ballet schools can be difficult and expensive – even before the lengthy audition proceedures.

The application process for ballet schools usually involves sending an application form, audition fee and photographs in certain ballet positions. Applicants are offered an initial audition: this could be a ballet class or up to a full day of dance classes and assessments, incorporating styles such as jazz.

For some schools, this initial round is all that is required to make offers of places. However, most ballet schools either run a second set of auditions or a scholarship round, unveiling more in-depth assessments. These can include another ballet class, solos, jazz class, tour of the school, physiotherapy assessment, interview or an academic test – each ballet school has a unique process.

This information is as accurate as possible at the time of writing. Please check each school's or organisation's website for the most up-to-date information.

To help make sense of the many options available to prospective students, Dancewear Central, which specialises in attire, compiled a guide to some of the UK's ballet schools, with ages ranging from 8 years old up to 16+ dance degree courses:

Elmhurst Ballet School

Ages accepted: 11-16 years and 16+   Birmingham, West Midlands

Formerly known as Elmhurst School for Dance, Elmhurst Ballet School (in association with Birmingham Royal Ballet) is the oldest vocational dance school in the UK. The school was originally based in Camberley, Surrey, but relocated to Birmingham in 2004. The school is based on a five-acre campus and include seven dance studios, a theatre workshop, a 250-seat studio theatre, medical centre and physiotherapy/exercise centre. The school's association with Birmingham Royal Ballet benefits many students, with opportunities to appear in the company's productions.

The school has an excellent success rate with graduates working with Birmingham Royal Ballet, The Royal Ballet, Northern Ballet, Scottish Ballet, Ballet Black, plus dance companies across Europe, USA and Japan.

Elmhurst acknowledges the risk of a dance career being potentially cut short by injury, and so they offer strong academic tuition. In their 2018 GCSE results, 90% of students received five Grades 9-4 (equivalent to A**-C), and 51% of these were Grade 7,8 and 9 (A/A*/A**). Students in sixth form can study A Levels, with a small number of students accepting places at universities following graduation from Elmhurst. In 2018, there was a 100% pass rate at A Level, with 85% gaining A*-C.

https://www.elmhurstdance.co.uk

The Hammond School

Ages accepted: 11-16 years and 16+   Chester, Cheshire

Established in 1917, The Hammond School offers specialist training courses in dance, drama and music for 11-16 year olds and dance, drama, music and musical theatre for ages 16+. The School is based in Hoole Bank House, built in the 1860s, and now has a Performing Arts Centre (with 420-seat theatre), dance studios and a music suite.

Most students sit up to 10 GCSEs, and students in the sixth form can also take a range of A Level subjects; the school was rated as outstanding in all categories by Ofsted. For students who do not wish to study A Levels, or have already completed them, the school offers alternative options such as Pilates Level 1 Mat Teaching Qualification, Zumba classes or fitness training. Sixth-form students study for a Level 6 Diploma, validated by Trinity College, London.

The school also offers a prep school for entry at Year 3; applications are welcome from all children, particularly those who demonstrate skill in the performing arts.

Dance students from the school have graduated into companies such as English National Ballet, Phoenix Dance Theatre, The Australian Ballet, Lithuanian National Opera and Ballet and Sir Matthew Bourne's New Adventures, dance theatre company.

https://www.thehammondschool.co.uk

Legat Dance Academy

Ages accepted: 11-16 years and 16+   Upper Dicker, East Sussex

The school offers intensive vocational dance training, with excellent tuition in academic subjects. It is based within the established St. Bede's School (which offers a nursery, prep school and senior school).

The school boasts a Manor House, with surrounding buildings including St. Bede's Recital Room, Science Block and Lakeside Classrooms – 'The Park' even has its own ornamental lake and island. Of importance to Legat dance students, the school has a 400-seat studio theatre. Students at the school train in classical ballet technique and its repertoire, contemporary dance technique and repertoire, improvisation, choreography, fitness and Pilates, alongside RAD examinations.

Director of Legat, Sherrie Pennington, trained at Laine Theatre Arts, Epsom, Surrey, UK.

http://www.bedes.org/legat.bedes.org/legat

Moorland School

Ages accepted: 8-11 years, 11-16 years and 16+ Clitheroe, Lancashire

Moorland International Ballet Academy is set in the beautiful grounds of Moorland School, based in the Ribble Valley. The school offers ballet training from Pre-Vocational (for ages 8-11) through to a Graduate Programme.

Moorland School, an academic school for Early Years children to sixth form, has outstanding academic results in GCSE, BTEC and A Level that places it in the top 1% of all British academic institutions. The school also hosts The Moorland Football Academy.

Moorland School is a non-selective school: students are instead invited to spend a day at the school, allowing staff to meet each child individually. There is no entrance exam; the school states that their entry requirements are based on behaviour. However, audition is required for the ballet academy.

Students of the international ballet academy train in classical ballet technique, repertoire, choreography, drama, anatomy and physiology, pointe work, virtuosity, contemporary dance, Spanish dance, Pilates, body conditioning and jazz. Students can also study for ISTD Cecchetti Vocational Grades, with the option of working towards teaching exams with the ISTD (the school is an ISTD Approved Dance Centre). Students of the school frequently compete at international competitions, such as Youth America Grand Prix, reputedly the world's largest ballet competition and scholarship programme.

https://moorlandandballetacademy.com

The Royal Ballet School (White Lodge)

Ages accepted: 11-16 years Richmond, London
and *16+* at The Upper School in Covent Garden, London

Originally the Sadler's Wells Ballet School, the Royal Ballet School is an internationally-acclaimed training school, producing some of the world's top dancers.

White Lodge, the boarding school for 11-16 year olds, is a former hunting lodge based in Richmond Park in London – competition is tough to gain a place at this prestigious school. Students at White Lodge have strong ties with the Royal Ballet School Upper School and also with the Royal Ballet, with their students frequently appearing in company productions.

The Royal Ballet School's White Lodge needs little introduction as a training school for ballet. White Lodge also has excellent academic results; in 2015/2016, 98% of the school's GCSE results were A*-C.

The Royal Ballet School Upper School is based in Covent Garden, and offers a three-year training course for students aged 16-19. Students study for a BA degree in Classical Ballet and Dance Performance, validated by the University of Roehampton. Students can study for A Levels alongside intensive classical ballet training.

Twelve of the Royal Ballet School graduates joined the Royal Ballet companies in 2018, and nine joined companies across Britain and the rest of the world.

https:www.royalballetschool.org.uk

Tring Park School for the Performing Arts

Ages accepted: 8-11 years, 11-16 years and 16+ Tring, Hertfordshire

Tring Park is a well-established performing arts school, accepting students from Preps (ages 8-11) up to and including sixth form (ages 16-19). For ages 11-14 (Juniors), Tring offer two courses: Junior Dance Course and Theatre Arts Course. In fourth and fifth form (ages 14-16), students can train on the Senior Dance Course or Performance Foundation Course.

Junior students take three and a half hours of dance classes each morning, followed by academic tuition in the afternoon. Middle School and Senior School take academic classes in the morning, followed by dance training in the afternoon.

At sixth form, students can choose from four courses: Dance, Acting, Musical Theatre, and operates Commercial Music and General Music. The school operates a flexible academic programme in sixth form where students can either concentrate on their vocational studies or study performing arts alongside an academic programme. Dance students in the sixth form study the Trinity National Diploma in Professional Dance and, in the final year, join the school's UK touring dance company, Encore Dance, under Artistic Director Antony Dowson.

Tring is well established within the dance industry and has a glittering list of alumni, with many students going on to careers in top ballet companies, West End shows, film and TV productions.

https://www.tringpark.com

Northern Ballet School

Ages accepted: 16+ years only Manchester, Lancashire

Based in the bustling heart of Manchester city centre, Northern Ballet School offers a three-year dance programme. The first year covers general dance training while, in the second and third year, students can choose to focus on classical ballet or jazz. Students can also gain ISTD teaching qualifications while at the school.

The school, based in a 1930s Art Deco building, has spacious studios with sprung floors and a 420-seat public theatre (The Dancehouse). The school has its own in-house ballet company, Manchester City Ballet, giving students the chance to perform full-length ballets.

Upon graduation, students receive the Northern Ballet School Diploma in Professional Dance, which incorporates the National Diploma in Professional Dance, validated by Trinity College of London.

Please note that Northern Ballet School, Manchester, is not linked to Northern Ballet, the ballet company based in Leeds.

http://www.northernballetschool.co.uk

Central School of Ballet

Ages accepted: 16+ years only Clerkenwell, London

Central School of Ballet, founded in 1982, is widely recognised for it's high level of training. Students receive training in ballet, contemporary dance, jazz dance, choreography, drama, music, singing and contextual studies.

Students at Central can take a two-year Foundation and BA (Hons) Degree in Professional Dance and Performance, validated by the University of Kent. The school also has a touring company for their final-year students, providing the opportunity to gain experience of professional life as a dancer.

In 2018, graduates secured contracts with Northern Ballet, Scottish Ballet, Matthew Bourne's New Adventures, Milwaukee Ballet II, Phantom of the Opera, Pécsi Belett, New English Ballet Theatre, Kibbutz Contemporary Dance Company, Cinevox, Opera Comica Pentru Copii, Mannheim Ballet and Baltic Opera.

https://www.centralschoolofballet.co.uk

English National Ballet School

Ages accepted: 16+ years only Royal Borough of Kensington and Chelsea, London

The school was founded in 1988 by English National Ballet to train students for a professional career in dance. Today the School exists as a separate entity but maintains strong links with its parent company, a touring ballet company with more than 60 dancers, sharing its commitment to excellence and access.

The course consists of daily ballet classes, pointe work, virtuosity, pas de deux, repertoire and variations, character dance, Pilates, contemporary classes (Graham and Cunningham technique), specialist coaching and individual training. The school also offers a Choreographic Course and Choreographic Competition.

Students are entered for the Diploma in Professional Dance (at Level 5 or 6), accredited by Trinity College, London. Upon graduation, however, students have the opportunity to take a one-year distance-learning course at Middlesex University in order to convert their Diploma into a Bachelor of Arts degree in Professional Practice.

In the second year, students have the chance to perform in English National Ballet's apprentice touring company; students tour the United Kingdom and are coached by English National Ballet artistic staff.

http://www.enbschool.org.uk

Rambert School of Ballet and Contemporary Dance

Ages accepted: 16+ years only Twickenham, London

The name Rambert is synonymous with contemporary dance and, as such, Rambert School is widely recognised for its outstanding contemporary dance training. Alumni are currently dancing in Rambert, Balletboyz, New Adventures, Phoenix Dance Theatre, Richard Alston Dance Company, Mark Bruce Company and Shobana Jeyasingh Dance Company, to name but a few.

The school's Foundation/BA (Hons) Degree course incorporates strong classical ballet technique. There are daily ballet and pointe work classes, along with pas de deux classes. These complement tuition in Graham and Cunningham techniques. By third year, students are versatile and prepared for graduation, having encountered many different styles of contemporary dance.

The school also has a Screening, Treatment and Rehabilitation Unit for body conditioning and Pilates.

https://www.rambertschool.org.uk

School of Ballet Theatre UK

Ages accepted: 16+ years only Hinckley, Leicestershire

School of Ballet Theatre UK is associated with international dance company Ballet Theatre UK. The course lasts three years: years one and two are spent studying for a BTEC Level 5 HND Diploma in Performing Arts

(QCF) and year three for a BA (Hons) Ballet Performance (in partnership with University of West London).

Students receive classical ballet training, pointe work, men's technique, virtuosity, pas de deux, repertoire and variations, contemporary dance (Cunningham and Graham techniques) and technical jazz.

Students take dance classes in state-of-the-art studios, and the school also offers housing exclusively for Ballet Theatre UK students. Students have gone on to careers in The Royal Ballet, Birmingham Royal Ballet, English National Ballet, American Ballet Theatre, Paris Opera Ballet and Matthew Bourne's New Adventures.

http://www.btukschool.com

Dance in schools

DDMIX for Schools was created by Dame Darcey Bussell DBE
Website: https://ddmixforschools.com/

Movement to music makes children come alive and changes the way they feel. With the DDMIX (diverse dance mix) programme, kids get an exciting and diverse learning experience that is physical and aerobic. It follows national curriculum PE guidelines.

Training is provided along with Schemes of Work for KS1 and KS2 to every teacher to deliver straightforward, fun and active PE lessons.

Organisations for other dance styles

The International Dance Organization (IDO) was founded as a non-profit organization on September 18, 1981 by Mr. Moreno Polidori, in Florence, Italy. The original founding member nations were Italy, France, Switzerland and Gibraltar. Mr. Polidori was appointed General Secretary and drew up the original statutes, by-laws and rules that governed the organization.

The **IDO** is not only involved with the granting of continental and international competitions and championships, but is deeply involved with many aspects of the dance industry. It is constantly striving to improve the quality of its dancers, through participation, its adjudicators through education, and national member images by being involved with the largest dance organisation in the world. The various disciplines, through their committees, are convened on a regular basis to ensure that the **IDO** rules are always current and up to date with its membership wishes.

Website: https://www.ido-dance.com/ceis/webHomeIdo.do
Email: info@ido-dance.com

Folk Dancing

The Country Dance and Song Society (CDSS) is an American non-profit organisation that seeks to promote participatory dance, music, and song with English and North American roots. Its vision statement is 'Communities strengthened by dancing, singing, and making music together.'

Website: https://www.cdss.org

Ballet/Contemporary/Jazz

The American Dance Guild (A.D.G.) was founded in 1956,as the Dance Teachers' Guild by twelve dance teachers in New York City to promote the art of dance in the United States by educating the American public and by maintaining standards of teaching. It is an annual conference on teaching children creatively. The conference provides teachers with a way to share ideas, problems and resources. The group meets and discusses the need to develop standards for teaching modern dance and ballet, and the need to educate the public about dance. It welcomes dance professionals.

Website: https://www.americandanceguild.org

Street Dancing

United Dance Organisation (UDO) Is a street dance organisation established in 2002. It is the world's largest international street dance movement, and fastest growing street, hip hop and commercial dance brand globally. UDO has 85,000 members across 30 countries including Australia, UAE, Germany, Japan, USA, Thailand, New Zealand, The Netherlands, and some in Africa.

UDO's mission is to provide dancers of all ages, levels, backgrounds, abilities and disabilities, a positive and supportive platform to unleash their creativity and passion. It believes in making street, hip hop and commercial dance inclusive for all. Whether dancing for fun, fitness, or with the aim of training to become a professional dancer, UDO's vision is to empower and inspire young people by nurturing skills, confidence, and talent in a safe and encouraging environment.

Website: www.udostreetdance.com

Ballroom (including Dance Sport)

• British Dance Council: https://www.britishdancecouncil.com

• Canadian Amateur DanceSport Association: http://www.dancesport.ca

• English Amateur Dancesport Association: http://www.eada.co.uk

• European Tournament for Dancing Students: http://www.etds.eu

• Swedish Dancsport Federation: https://www.danssport.se

• World Dance Council: https://www.wdcdance.com

• World DanceSport Federation: https://www.worlddancesport.org

Country and Western

• United Country Western Dance Council: https://ucwdc.org

Rock'n'Roll, Modern Jive, Swing

• World Rock'n'Roll Confederation: https://wrrc.dance

Dance for Parkinson's and Dementia

• **East London Dance**

Dance for Prevention-Health and well-being objective led project.

Website: https://www.eastlondondance.org

• **Green Candle Dance**

Community Dance in London

Website: https:/www.greencandledance.com

• **Mindfulness**

Mindfulness Journey Workshops delivered virtually.

Practising mindfulness reduces stress and anxiety, improves memory, and promotes empathy.

Participants learn unique mindfulness practices that incorporate into their daily lives. Increase productivity, facilitate a work-life balance and reduce stress.

Saskia Meckman - BA,MIIM, RYT

saskia.meckman@gmail.com Telephone in USA +1 617-306-4131

Ballet Companies

The list of ballet companies in the world is extremely long to include here but you may wish to use the link below. You will find details of a myriad of dance companies worldwide, many of whom offer classes, workshops, and of course performances.

https://www.danceonline.co.uk/list-of-dance-companies.html
and
http://www.balletcompanies.com (scroll down and click on country)

Children waiting to attend a ballet workshop at
the Royal Academy of Dance in London

Afterword

Congratulations on reaching the end of this whirlwind tour around all the joys and benefits of dance! I hope you can see dance isn't just an activity that other people do, or reserved for weddings and parties. Rather that it's something that can bring joy to your life, and your family's life, every day or week.

Put simply, I believe dance can help you live well. And that is why I want as many people as possible to read this book. Please pass on your copy if you know someone who would appreciate it.

I also believe dance is essential to our society. We have evidence that dancing was a feature of early civilisations. It is social communication, it is beautiful expression, it is joyful celebration of our lives, our bodies and our communities. It was then, and it is now. Our dance bonds and friendships often are for life. Children and adults who started their dancing journey with me inevitably have lifelong cherished friends.

Dance has always been part of my life, and I am extraordinarily grateful. Since my working life started in earnest, I have been fully employed within the dance world in one way or another. I have had such wonderful experiences through life and people tell me that it is keeping me young – which is why I found myself working full-time heading a programme at a dance school in my seventies and teaching Silver Swans.

I know not everyone has had the same opportunity to dance as I have. Dance may be something that has only been at the edges of your life. Maybe you ruled yourself out of any dancing activity because you didn't fit your own stereotypes of who dancers are.

I hope this book helps you to see that dance also belongs to you, and your children. All it takes is for you to say yes and to move your body. If there is a particular style you are drawn to, seek out a teacher. If you would rather dance at home, put on some music and do that. If you want to encourage your children to dance more and have fun, do it first. Show them rather than tell them. Be the role model they need.

The Covid-19 pandemic and lockdowns showed us there are no barriers to dance. We can dance in our kitchens, on football fields, on balconies – anywhere works! And we no longer need to go to dance studios for tuition – the miracles of technology bring tutors straight into our living space.

There are no prizes for how you choose to take up dancing, aside from the intrinsic rewards dance provides in itself. Your mind and body will thank you, whatever you do.

Life is full of exciting opportunities, so step forward and take them. So, I suggest if you feel inspired to dance or to encourage others to, you must go ahead. Say yes to yourself and do it.

Allow yourself to commit to dancing, even if it's just for half an hour a week. Do this for three months and keep a note of how you feel. Think about your mood, your fitness and your connection to other people. I'd love to hear the impact it has on you.

suehewgillpeterson101@gmail.com

As I mentioned in the introduction, this book is written in support of the *We Can Dance* charity, which provides dance opportunities for children with special needs. The teachers and students in those classes truly embody the spirit of dancing. They have fun, persevere, they make new friends. They use their creativity, they learn. They surprise themselves, and those around them, by doing more than they thought possible.

If they can do it. You can do it.

I'll leave you with these words…

We Can Dance!

Happy Dancing!

A Dancer's Life

First Position

A little girl who's only three
(I think that little girl was me)
With shining eyes and ringlets curled
Was shown into a magic world.

Second Position

Now getting honours in grade Five
Why – that's what made me feel alive
Back aching, bones and all my joints,
At last I rise upon my pointes!

Third Position

And now I am a working girl
My work? Well, I spin and twirl.
My toes all bleed, I'm hot and sweaty
But I sure can do a mean fouetté!

Fourth Position

Grown up , and doing other things,
I now discard my fairy wings
Hang up my pointe shoes for the day
And send dancing on its merry way

Fifth Position

So now I've got my bus pass – I thought why not have a go?
I'll join an adult ballet class and relive all those years ago
My legs remember what to do - they just don't go as high
But when I'm doing pose turns – my god – I really fly!

So never forget to do the thing
You find is life enhancing;
Dust off your tights and spend your nights
Dancing, dancing, dancing!!.

*Written by **Lesley North** 2017   My school friend of many dancing years*

The *A Dancer's Life* poem is thought provoking, it reminds us of so many little girls' ideas of a dancer. The story also brings tears to my eyes because additionally it reminds me of another long-time school friend who choreographed a beautiful dance when she was training. She recreated it and it was her swan song. It depicts the five positions that are the basis of ballet. Miss Sue Robinson dedicated her life to Ballet and Dance but sadly lost her life to cancer. She gifted the joy of dance and music to so many dancers, boys and girls, and now will be teaching the stars to dance.

Five Positions, choreographed by Sue when we were at Elmhurst Ballet School, then in Camberley, Surrey, England and reproduced here for her pupils (only a fifty plus year gap but just as fresh and appealing!). It showed the talent she revealed way back in school and went on to make so much of during her illustrious career. The particularly interesting thing is that Annik Coatalen, our school friend, was in the original piece as the Fifth position dancer.

This photo is from 2017. Sue and Annik are discussing the production of *Five Positions* in one of the studios in the new buildings of Elmhurst moved in 2004 to Birmingham. It was originally in the performance of *Swish of Blue Velvet* when Annik performed *Five Positions* in the 1960s. Looking on are their students.

A funny and interesting story about Fred Astaire.
After his first audition in Hollywood he was told:

Can't sing, can't act, going bald, can dance a little.

But see what he achieved in his life!

Learn to DANCE!
Enjoy!
Be proud of your achievements.

Firstly, thank you to my long-suffering husband, Jerry, who supports me in all things Ballet and Dance. Most especially with this book. This book is a bringing together ideas and stories from many people and wouldn't be so powerful without them.

I am grateful to my neighbour Ann, who suggested the name Dance for your Life, she also assisted with editing. Julia, my friend in Wales who helped me coin the phrase… change life in a **D a n c e b e a t !**

Granddaughters Pria worked on many aspects of detailed research Anoushka drew pictures and granddaughter Sally made a picture too.

Daughter Joy has always been a wealth of advice, great suggestions and generally typing speedily which is not my forte. She chose the front cover.

Former pupil Charlie Dickenson for her incomparable advice and encouragement.

All friends and family who endure my hectic lifestyle!

Jessica Spencer-Keyse for being there during the first tentative steps. Gayle Johnson for assistance with writing.

Thanks to Richard Powers who gave permission November 14, 2021, for his article Use It or Lose It: Dancing Makes You Smarter, Longer. July 30, 2010. Copyright © 2010, 2015 Richard Powers, Chapter 6.

Thank you Dancewear Central, a renowned Dancewear shop in Blackpool commissioned an article by Faye Nash for their website, have kindly agreed to share it. *www.dancewearcentral.co.uk/blog/6-things-children-learn-in-dance-class-that-are-not-dancing* Chapter 3. Also, The Schools Guide in the final chapter.

Thanks to Mother and daughter team, Claire and Barbara who are immensely passionate about babyballet© and have worked tirelessly since 1999 to make it into the award-winning reputable concept it is today. Chapter 4.

Thanks for permission from Steve Sirico from the Dance Teacher Web, A Tribute to Dance Teachers and Studio Owners Everywhere! You can find it in Chapter 8. I just had to include it. It was written in 2021.

Edwin Diaz, Daily Mail reporter, gave permission to quote from his article in Chapter 5. Andrew Self gave permission for his inclusion in Chapter 7 The photo is credited to photographer Alex Rumford - it was taken at the Mousetrap Theatre Projects awards in May 2019.

June Lawrence, Assistant to Rhee Gold says he would be pleased for you to use .
his quote For me Dance is Life. Chapter 2.

Debbie McGee for becoming involved.

Iain Webb, Margaret Barbieri and Christopher Hird of The Sarasota Ballet in Florida, USA.

Paul James of Birmingham Royal Ballet for use of photo.

Jan Masters and the Telegraph Syndication Department. Article courtesy of Telegraph
Media Group Ltd.

Toni Renee Taylor thank you for permission to use lovely photos.

Thank you Dr Merritt Moore, for inspiring insights into space. Also, Universal Robots for
photos. Thanks to photographer Skjalg Vold for permission to use his photo. Visit his
website to see his amazing portfolio: *www.skjalgvold.com*.

Dame Darcey Bussell for information about DDMIX.

Dr Dance, Dr Peter Lovatt, author of "The Dance Cure", for his encouragement.

Thank you to 'Cherie Belly Dancer', a professional belly dancer who kindly gave permission
to use the photo on p. 122. Visit her website for more information: *www.cheriebellydancer.com*.

Lastly, I have my biggest thank you to very special people. They are all a Godsend.

Helen Senior who has tirelessly worked on designing and producing this visually beautiful
book. She has kept calm and given invaluable advice. Her drawings are awesome too.
Helen is an experienced book designer having worked in the publishing industry for nearly
40 years. She has worked for prestigious companies including Penguin, Collins, and Dorling
Kindersley (DK), where she was the Children's Creative Director until moving to Suffolk to
freelance. She can be contacted at *helenseniordesign@gmail.com*.

Matt George who assisted with editing and proof reading in a very sympathetic and
thought-provoking way. Nasreen Hammond for fabulous back up and proof reading.

Thanks to the following of the Royal Academy of Dance: Melanie Murphy, Director of
Marketing and Communications, Luke Rittner (recently retired Chief Executive) and
Tim Arthur, Chief Executive for his uplifting and inspiring 'Foreword'.

Last, but not least, my brothers: Jeremy who encouraged me all along, His experience with
publishing has been invaluable and Peter for overall support. I shall always be grateful to
my parents, Jasper and Margaret Rudd, for supporting me through my Ballet and Dance
career from age 3 which has given me such a rich and interesting life.

Picture credits

Cover and p155: AlexanderNovikov/iStock.com

Title page: Leila/stock.adobe.com

Contents page: Prostock-studio/stock.adobe.com

Page 4: Market Hill Photography

Page 5: Bushell and Sons, Henley on Thames

Page 6: *Anne Walker* - Stu Booth, *Sandra Burnham* - David Tett

Page 7: *Kathi Doepfner* - own photo *Lynn Gregory* - own photo

Page 10: Sue Hewgill Peterson

Page 12/13: Rzoog/stock.adobe.com

Page 14: Simple miracle/stock.adobe.com

Page 15: Maria Moroz/stock.adobe.com, *Background:* caanebez/stock.adobe.com

Page 16: kowit/stock.adobe.com

Page 17: Dex Honea at Vuttiphotography

Page 18: Leila/stock.adobe.com, *Background:* BoszyArtis/stock.adobe.com

Page 19: Leila/stock.adobe.com

Page 21: Flamingo images/stock.adobe.com

Page 22/3: KtsanaBlue/stock.adobe.com

Page 24: *Abi Murray* - own photo

Page 26: *Ballerina:* Simple line/stock.adobe.com, *Pencil:* Modisketch/stock.adobe.com

Page 28: brooke-cagle/Unsplash.com

Page 30: John Green © Dover Publications

Page 31: Pressmaster/stock.adobe.com

Page 32: Flamingo images/stock.adobe.com

Page 32/3: *Background:* artemisia1508/stock.adobe.com

Page 35: Andrew Barton

Page 36: Sue Hewgill Peterson

Page 39: R. Gaskell, Darwen, N Yorkshire

Page 41: Konradbak/stock.adobe.com

Page 42: Simple miracle/stock.adobe.com

Page 43: sanjoy-sadhukhan/Unsplash.com

Page 44: Freepik.com *Background:* Caanebez/stock.adobe.com

Page 49: Cassie Cooper

Page 51: Alpha27/stock.adobe.com

Page 54/5: Africa studio/stock.adobe.com *Background:* Niko180180/stock.adobe.com

Page 56: Simple miracle/stock.adobe.com

Page 57: Freepik.com

Page 58: Ron Francis

Page 59: Simple line/stock.adobe.com

Page 61: Sue Hewgill Peterson

Page 62: Brian Slater, courtesy of Royal Academy of Dance

Page 67: Babyballet

Page 66/7: *Background:* artemisia1508/stock.adobe.com

Page 66: Sue Hewgill Peterson

Page 71: Skjalg Vold

Page 72: Kowi/stock.adobe.com

Page 73: fizkes/iStock.com

Page 75: WavebreakMedisMicro/stock.adobe.com

Page 76: Simple miracle/stock.adobe.com

Page 78: Viacheslav Lakobchuk/stock.adobe.com

Page 80: Maureen Dye

Page 81: Barbara Peters

Page 82: Babyballet

Page 83: Jason Akira Jhung, Ninja Pirate Productions

Page 84: Roy Similjanic

Page 85: *top:* Frank Atura *bottom:* Libby Christensen

Page 86: kowit/stock.adobe.com

Page 87: gift-habeshaw/Unsplash.com

Page 88: Kateryna Kovarzh/stock.adobe.com

Page 90/1: ktsana/stock.adobe.com

Page 92: *Social:* tangolf/stock.adobe.com

Competitive: befree/stock.adobe.com, Victoria VIAR PRO/stock.adobe.com

Exhibition: Victoria VIAR PRO/stock.adobe.com

Page 98: ardian-lumi-6Woj_wozqmA/Unsplash.com

Page 100/1: Drobot Dean/Unsplash.com

Page 102: Simple Line/ stock.adobe.com

Page 103: Marc Thorneycroft/Photoworks

Page 104: Alex Rumford

Page 105: Frank Atura

Page 111: Pip Marsh

Page 112: *top:* simple line/stock.adobe.com

bottom: Armes Photography

Page 114/115: Elnur/stock.adobe.com

Page 117: Jan Masters

Page 119: Leila/stock.adobe.com

Page 120/1: artemis/stock.adobe.com

Page 121: majoros166/stock.adobe.com

Page 122: Andy Wick/Oakmist Photography

Page 123: darkbird/stock.adobe.com *Background:* caanebez/stock.adobe.com

Page 125: Coka/stock.adobe.com

Page 127: BoszyArtis/stock.adobe.com

Page 128: Sorcha Augustine - sorchaaugustine.com

Page 130: Racool_studio/Freepik.com

Page 130/31/32: Magdalena/stock.adobe.com

Page 133: chermiti-mohamed-8dRFHIkhukc/Unsplash.com

Page 149: Joan Bradford

Page 150: Anoushka Mani

Page 152/3: Юлия Завалишина/stock.adobe.com

Page 154: Sue Hewgill Peterson

Lightning Source UK Ltd.
Milton Keynes UK
UKHW020943090922
408549UK00001B/17